THE
FUTURE
ANCESTOR

THE
FUTURE
ANCESTOR

THE
FUTURE
ANCESTOR

A Guide and Journey
to Oneness

ANNABELLE SHARMAN

HAY HOUSE

Carlsbad, California • New York City
London • Sydney • New Delhi

Published in the United Kingdom by:
Hay House UK Ltd, The Sixth Floor, Watson House
54 Baker Street, London W1U 7BU
Tel: +44 (0)20 3927 7290; Fax: +44 (0)20 3927 7291; www.hayhouse.co.uk

Published in the United States of America by:
Hay House Inc., PO Box 5100, Carlsbad, CA 92018-5100
Tel: (1) 760 431 7695 or (800) 654 5126; Fax: (1) 760 431 6948 or (800) 650 5115
www.hayhouse.com

Published in Australia by:
Hay House Australia Ltd, 18/36 Ralph St, Alexandria NSW 2015
Tel: (61) 2 9669 4299; Fax: (61) 2 9669 4144; www.hayhouse.com.au

Published in India by:
Hay House Publishers India, Muskaan Complex, Plot No.3, B-2,
Vasant Kunj, New Delhi 110 070
Tel: (91) 11 4176 1620; Fax: (91) 11 4176 1630; www.hayhouse.co.in

A catalogue record for this book is available from the British Library.

Tradepaper ISBN: 978-1-4019-6827-4
Ebook ISBN: 978-1-78817-795-5
Audiobook ISBN: 978-1-78817-789-4

Interior illustrations: 1, 61, 109, 145, 177: artwork 'Paika' by Emma-Jayde Chapman,
concept by Annabelle Sharman; all other illustrations © Annabelle Sharman

Printed in the United States of America

10 9 8 7 6 5 4 3 2 1

For Emily.

CONTENTS

Contents

FOREWORD

If you look up the word 'nature' in the dictionary you'll find many things referenced, including plants, stones, animals and landscapes. You'll also find that it doesn't just leave out humans, it specifically states that humans aren't part of nature, they're separate to it.

Is it any wonder that so many of us feel disconnected and that our lives have become compartmentalized? How so many in the West have seen the land as something to own and conquer? How we as humans have caused so much harm to this planet (and each other) rather than seeing ourselves as an extension of it? How spirituality has, for many, become separate from the Earth?

Indigenous earth-based traditions have always seen the Earth and all beings as interconnected and sacred. Humans as one with the Earth itself. Interconnected. The sacred, carefully woven within, in all beings and all things.

For many, the sacred is something separate from our everyday life. Spirituality and nature are compartmentalized. It's as if we've forgotten to see the sacred thread that's so fully woven into all of Life and all of nature. And we've forgotten that we don't just exist in nature, rather we, too, are nature. Many have been severed from the earth-based wisdom teachings and wise ones of our ancestry. Perhaps it's this severing that's caused so much harm to humanity, each other, ourselves and the Earth. Perhaps it's this disconnection that's caused so much persecution, especially to the indigenous peoples of the world.

We're finally waking up to the urgent realization that we've created a world on top of the world. We've been seeking the sacred someplace else, some place other than here, as if it's something to work towards, some destination to arrive at. Indigenous elders and wise ones know that the sacred is right here, on Earth, in the trees and the flowers, the rocks and the animals, the sun and the sky. From star to seed, sea to cell, the sacred has always been right here, within all beings and all things.

In this beautiful, thought-provoking book, Annabelle invites us to open our eyes to the reality of where we are both personally and collectively in order for true healing to happen. Guided by the whispers of her ancestors, Annabelle provides a steady, simple path for true healing and hope for the world, for humanity and for ourselves, without bypassing anything. A gifted storyteller, Annabelle shares in a way that transports you to the campfire with a cuppa between your hands, the red dirt underfoot and the Murray lapping in the distance, regulating your nervous system like a mother rocking her child. You can almost smell her famous pumpkin soup brewing in the distance and see her huge Spirit Cloth pot slowly alchemizing on the fire. Chapter by chapter, she invites us to slow down, listen, unwind, experience YUMA and truly be.

The Future Ancestor is a call to see the sacred in the everyday, and to develop a conscious relationship with the land that holds, sustains and nurtures us. It's a clear call to action to own our story, personally and culturally, and to heal what's ours to heal so that, ultimately, we can take our place as ancestors for those yet to come.

I'm a white Australian woman who grew up on land different from my ancient ancestry (Garigal and Gannagal land). As a child I felt deeply connected to the earth and heard the whispers, yet I felt an ache that I wasn't able to describe. This ache resulted in me boarding a plane at the age of 19 to embark on a solo pilgrimage to the lands of my ancestry, the place where I currently live. I was in my fourth decade before I could put words around what this ache was – it was a separation from the culture that saw the sacred and the earth as one, a lack of reverence to the sacred in the everyday, and something that was either external to aspire to, or not important. For as long as I can remember I've longed for a direct experience of the sacred right here, rather than as something outside of myself. After dedicating my life to the sacred and since unpacking the devastating effects of colonialism, it saddens me that the rich wisdom of the Aboriginal people (and the majority of the world's indigenous traditions) has not been cherished, protected and revered. And this is just one of the many reasons why this book you're holding in your hands is so important.

I believe that many of us have an ache, deep down, to experience the sacred in the everyday. To re-weave the thread all the way back in. From chapter to chapter, this is what Annabelle does. As the Spirit Weaver, from story to channelled poetic whispers, Annabelle encourages and empowers us to own our unique story and to weave our own metaphoric Spirit Cloth.

She invites us to turn our gaze down and inwards, to experience YUMA and remember how to just be. She teaches us again and again that the sacred is right here, on Earth, woven through every moment and everything – the swaying gum trees and the dry rugged stones, the rich red sands and the pure waters that sustain us. With colonialism and Westernization, so much sacred wisdom has been tragically lost and so much harm has been done. Yet in nature and through the ancestors, we can reach back and remember.

If you track back far enough, you'll likely find indigenous earth-based traditions in your ancestry. Wise ones who tended to the land and lived in reverence to the sacred woven through it all. And despite the tragic harm that colonialism and patriarchy have caused, there are still indigenous wisdom keepers (living and past) who hold this thread and sing us on. May we protect, support and revere them. May we listen deeply to their songs.

You've probably felt it already, but in your hands is a very important book whose time has certainly come. Annabelle Sharman has courageously stepped forward to be a voice of wisdom and healing in these severed times. With her poetic words of wisdom and charming Aussie humour, Annabelle takes us from laughter to tears, from deep peace to justified sacred rage in a matter of minutes. She goes deep, she keeps it real and she offers hope and a way forward for humanity.

Throughout the book we are transported back and forth from past to present to timeless time where the Sacred and the whispers of the ancestors reside. Read these words with your heart as there is wisdom from past, present and future seeded through them all.

The Healer and Shaman know that true healing isn't possible without facing what's been severed and broken. We can't truly move forward and live in the present without first acknowledging the past. Annabelle does not bypass the reality of where we are collectively and individually, and yet she offers seeds of hope for humanity and the planet as a whole.

This is such an important book for Australia and indeed for the world. My prayer is that as you read this book, you listen from your heart. If you do, you may just hear the ancestors, Grandmothers and wise ones through the ages who have forever been singing you on.

May we reach back through the ages to the ones who never forgot. May we listen to the stories of people who are different from our own. May we find the courage to face the past in order to mend what has been severed and broken. May we place our ear to the Earth and listen with an open heart, body and mind. May we protect the indigenous wisdom of the Earth, so much of which has been lost. And when the time is right, may we bravely take our place as a Future Ancestor of those yet to come.

Rebecca Campbell
Glastonbury, UK, 2022

INTRODUCTION

This book is an experience and journey to a sacred healing Soul Spirit space.

I am an Ancestor of the future.

Here I am, I have arrived.

I am here, I heard you.

I honour you, I honour me.

*I breathe and dance with my Ancestors
when I close my eyes and dream.*

*They guide me to create the Rhythm of Light to heal
Mother Earth, My People and Humanity.*

We are all Future Ancestors, and as a Future Ancestor we each have a responsibility to nurture, protect and restore the balance to our Mother (Earth). We are of her. She owns us. This book honours her and honours us.

Hi, I am Annabelle Sharman. I am a proud Aboriginal Bush woman of the Mutti Mutti tribe grown in the Australian Mallee among the gum trees, the Murray River and red dirt running through me. In this lifetime, I am (have become) the Spirit Weaver, living Self, Spirit and Mother Earth. I have become the Master of my own healing journey, having learned my lessons through life. I am a survivor and now I am Home, I am whole and I am Oneness.

As the Spirit Weaver, my Dreaming is to journey, connect, heal and bring people back home to their own Self, Spirit, heart and breath with grace, honour and peace so they may feel Oneness and live and practise YUMA.

YUMA empowers you to BE your own Healer and BE the Medicine in your personal Healing, Wellness and Dreaming Journey. YUMA is a Mutti Mutti language word meaning 'BE', and YUMA is my Dreaming to live in Oneness, to live and BE Self, Spirit and Mother Earth. My grandmother showed me and led me to YUMA. Grandmother's wisdom whispers are offered throughout the journey. I am now inviting you to be led too. To BE YUMA, you need to return home and remember Us as the Healer and the Medicine and living Self, Spirit and Mother Earth.

Throughout this book, I hold a space for you to see and feel through your Ancestor eyes, heart and Spirit and to dance through the pages of this book. You will be guided to uncover, unravel and discover a piece of who you truly are.

Society often forces you to search for happiness, love or life outside yourself. You may then have forgotten where your real home and sacred space is. *And that is within us.*

You may feel *lost*; I say you are *just returning*. This book will take you, the reader, on a journey back home so you can take your place as a Future Ancestor.

My message about being a Future Ancestor is not just about me being an Australian Aboriginal person or a grandmother, or for my people or my grandchildren. It is beyond that. It is Universal. It is about how we can all be better people and live in a new world, a better world.

ACKNOWLEDGEMENT OF COUNTRY - ANCESTORS

I honour all my Ancestors who Dreamed me into being and existence.

I acknowledge my Ancestral Homelands.

That of my Grandmother, the first people, the Aboriginal people of this country, Australia, and Grandfather and Father, the Māori people of New Zealand.

I have a strong sense of belonging, knowing and connection to the lands and waterways that have nurtured and sustained me on my journey to live in Oneness.

I will continue to walk with honour and strength and embody the Spirit of my Ancestors to empower hope, peace, freedom and healing.

I acknowledge that sovereignty was never ceded.

Always was and always will be Aboriginal land.

'We are bound through the weavings of our Ancestors; with their guidance we gain the knowledge and the strength to perceive all that was and all that will be.'

JESSICA SHARMAN

MY TRUTH

My name is Annabelle Sharman. I am a Grandmother, Bush woman, Healer, Writer, Visionary, Cultural Conservationist, Creative, Social Worker and Community Member from Robinvale in the Mallee of Victoria, Australia, where the Murray River flows through.

I am a proud Australian Aboriginal woman of the Mutti Mutti tribe, grown and raised in a large extended family among the gum trees, the Murray River and red dirt running through me. Fifty years of age is a long time and a lot of experiences, 'aha' moments, magical moments and moments where, by the grace of God, you felt so lucky, grateful and alive.

For me, my first memory was seeing through my eyes as a new baby, and my aunty and uncle reaching in to pick me up from a makeshift cot made in the bottom drawer of the cupboard. I can remember the exact location, the time of day and their faces. I can also remember and feel the love as I was scooped up from the drawer.

That love was woven through our large extended family to my other siblings, me being the youngest of 10 children. The kinship care in Aboriginal families is unique.

My mother's sister Aunty Lil and her husband, Uncle Buck, committed and dedicated their lives (as a young married couple with a young family of their own) to care for and raise her sister's kids. My mother had two marriages. Frank was her second husband and together they had five children. My mother, Phyllis, and father, Frank, died when I was a young toddler. My heart followed their love back and forward across two family homes, theirs and my sister's, across the connecting streets of Ronald and Kennedy, in the Mallee town of Robinvale.

However, when I remember now, Ronald Street was where the feelings of great trauma, grief, loss and abandonment are.

I call myself a Kennedy Street kid because that is where I grew and matured and was nurtured before I ventured out on my own at 16. I watched my aunty and uncle work daily jobs, my aunty for community service in Health and Education and my uncle as a gun (expert) picker of grapes and shearer of sheep with his crew alongside him. I absorbed that strong work and learning ethic from them. The greatest gift and lessons I could have received – a deep sense of inner strength, never giving up, being a strong Black independent woman. I am my mother and grandmother's Dreaming.

In this lifetime I have become the Spirit Weaver, living Self, Spirit and Mother Earth. I have become the Master of my own healing journey, having learned my own lessons through life. I am a survivor and now I am Home, am whole and I am Oneness. As the Spirit Weaver, my Dreaming is to journey, connect, heal and bring people back home to their own Self, Spirit, heart and breath with grace, honour and peace so they may feel Oneness.

I pay deep respect to the Mutti Mutti matrilineal lineage of my grandmother and her spiritual guidance, which I carry with me every day. Deep ancestral knowledge, Spirit and wisdom guide every part of my healing work. At this stage in my life – 50 laps around the sun – I feel I have mastered many things.

However, I now have set a deep challenge to master the sourdough. This 'new trend' reminds me of growing up with my sister and extended family and the smell of her famous damper being baked in the old wood-fired oven next to her pot of soup. The joy of smothering our hot damper with butter and golden syrup or dipping it in our soup. It reminds me that in times of uncertainty, we seek a remembering and reimaging of Old Ways.

I own lots of books and have kept a diary since I was 13 years old, writing and recording my life story and healing history as I go. I am now ready to share this with you, the reader. Many of my memories and experiences have emerged during the writing of this book. So many people close to me are hearing these stories for the first time too.

Social justice, having a voice and being heard, and challenging oppressive exploitive systems have been my life career as a Social Worker, Aboriginal girl, woman, mother and grandmother. I have been pushed and pulled to the brink over and over again for my voice to be heard – in my life, as a little girl, as an educated adult, as a professional and now as a Writer. I doubted and questioned myself, others questioned me and governments questioned me. In them wishing to silence me, I began to silence myself. So, feeling like a failed, half-assed Writer and Healer I almost gave up.

Of course, Ancestors and Spirit were not going to allow that to happen. Just as I was about to say 'Fuck this! Here we go again!' I heard the words of Cyndi Lauper's song 'Time After Time' playing, and I realized that if I felt myself falling, I would need to catch myself.

Wake up, Annabelle. This is real. This is your life; this is *your* experience. Follow your own authentic threads linking the standards and rules you have set out: not to write about, guide, encourage or advise others on any path I have not walked myself or experience I have not had. Gee, practise what you preach, sista! I have been telling my clients for 20 years: 'Tell your own story, write your own story, all stories are unique and important.' Truth-telling needs to be acknowledged, respected and celebrated.

This book is about my healing way and YUMA philosophy of Oneness, and Earth Medicine that is represented through the Spirit Cloth. It may sound confusing to some.

This is my Mystical.

This is Real.

This is Me.

I am Oneness. I am Self, Spirit and Mother Earth.

I will share and write about my Journey to Oneness in my most authentic healing way and take you on a walk so you, too, can experience the journey.

This book is an experience and journey to a sacred healing Soul Spirit space.

In writing this book of my own personal experiences, and unravelling the trauma and healing along the way, this book is writing itself. I am writing myself home.

> '*Diverse voices mean voices that are different to our own. Voices that may raise questions and possibly discomfort. That is the beauty of sharing stories in honesty. Expecting everything to be comfortable and recognizable is biased and shows white privilege.*
>
> *Black voices, diverse voices, have long been silenced and/or measured by white "standards". This is Othering. For true connection, honesty and difference are celebrated. We might have to work a bit harder, look within and reflect more. But the outcome is worth it, as it is authentic.*
>
> *This isn't a cookie-cutter book. It's an authentic journey that is grounded in lived and cultural experience.*'
>
> **DR MEAGHAN KATRAK-HARRIS**

In Oneness, we dance together to the rhythm of the gentle breath. Together we stoke the fire energy of Ancestors as we reconnect back into our bodies and back into our spiritual soundness.

We be in breath.

We be in the stillness of our body, in the quiet, in the calm, and deep down into the centre of our soulfulness.

We are interconnected with all that lives and breathes and with all that does not.

There is no separation. There is no division. We have a feeling and that is our knowing.

And all in one breath we are one, we are everything and we are nothing but Oneness.

PART ONE

Connection

This section is made up of the following chapters:

- Orphan Story – Who I to Be

- Petunias, Emily and Hope

- My Journey to Oneness

- Spirit Weaver

This section will reveal where my journey story was remembered, and how I woke up. And from this moment I felt alive – truly alive and breathing. I was resuscitated back to life and was moving in the same rhythm and vibrating with Mother Earth. I stepped out of the darkness.

This is where my human story begins.

While standing on the bare earth beside the magnificent Murray River, watching the Great Eagle fly overhead and catching a sudden whiff of eucalyptus through my senses, I knew something profoundly healing and life-changing was about to happen. My skin was dancing with joy, and I felt my body for the first time. The smoke circled me, and I was dancing and breathing with the Ancestors. I could smell the eucalyptus from the leaves placed on the flames; it smelled ancient and sacred. Very sacred. This was my first Ceremonial Smoking. My Soul Spirit was screaming for healing and to be found. I just had to stand still long enough and just BE to receive.

The thread of connection symbolizes the
medium that links all to One.

Sometimes we may become tangled, cut, loosened,
or frayed but what remains is the impact we
had on that connection at any one time.

The thread of connection links us to the now, to our future
and to our Ancients. It is the Soul, the Breath, the Spirit.

ORPHAN STORY – WHO I TO BE

*Together we are woven into the fabric that is our
life experiences. We are all interwoven. We are
all threaded together into the story that is the
Oneness. Together we form the tapestry of life.*

I have had recent memory bubbles burst their juicy nectar on me as I'm ready and guided by Spirit to write this book. My dreams remind me and guide my story.

I reconnected to a particular time in my childhood when I was gifted a 'Tweety-bird' in a cage at school, and I am now remembering its significance in my healing journey.

I didn't know I was an orphan. I didn't even know what it meant until the principal and another teacher told me at primary school. I was singled out, away from my best friend, Sissy, and feeling lonely as I stood in the hot summer sun along the breezeway. I can picture

5

it now, covered in ornamental grapevines with green sprinkles falling from its foliage. I was called 'Orphan Annie' at that moment in time. They told me this news and then gave me this present, a toy 'Tweety-bird' in a cage – the ones you have to wind up like a ballerina in a jewellery box. To me, it seemed that little Tweety-bird in that cage symbolized disconnection, locked up in a fucking cage and wound up when someone else needed to feel love. I would have preferred to have that ballerina, symbolizing moving with grace, dancing with the flow of life and, importantly, having freedom. That is my point! I didn't need that Tweety-bird.

I didn't need that Tweety-bird.

That Tweety-bird seemed to symbolize my life.

Being encaged, silenced and waiting for someone to give attention and care.

Being traumatized as a little girl, that little girl... that orphan little Black girl.

Dealing with being raped and abused through the night in silence by another young person from the town. Waiting, praying the night predator would not appear again through what I thought were locked doors and windows. Hoping someone would save me and my innocence. My voice was frozen. My body was frozen.

Silence turned into more silence.

Silence turned into more trauma.

This early event in my life was silenced within my being and almost forgotten about until I started deep healing and writing this book.

This trauma resulted in a lifetime of wanting to be safe, free, protected, loved and cared for.

As I moved through those childhood years, I often became sick with throat issues and was given lots of antibiotic medication. The backyard nectarine tree received those medications as I ceremonially buried all those tablets. I refused to put them in my body at that young age.

I didn't need them; I knew I didn't. That little girl's Soul Spirit knew she should not take them. From a young age, I embodied my Mother's Spirit of protection. As I know now, her energy and love were and became my personal Spirit Cloth, as will unfold in this story.

7

Then, however, I just needed to be heard and physically safe on this Earthly Plain.

The throat issues followed me through life. And later in life, I discovered why.

•••

Fifty years Earthside, I feel healed and heard from a very deep, deep part of my heart, and I can hear my own voice as I continue to write and tell these hidden stories. I have this strong sense of knowing when I am remembering the pain, the grief and the trauma of being a little Black girl living on Ronald Street in a small Mallee town and called Orphan Annie.

Under the Australian assimilation policies, Aboriginal children were still being forcibly removed from their families, now known as the 'Stolen Generation'. I remember being fed, spoiled and friended by white neighbours and family friends. I was more aware of the meaning of orphan since the 'Tweety-bird' gift. I was possibly seven or eight years old. I ate many treats and remembered their words so clearly after being given many servings of ice cream and pancakes and yummy snacks. 'Do you want to live with us? We want to adopt you.' I guess they were sorry for me, this little innocent Black girl, and wanted a better-privileged future for me.

From this point on, I remember not visiting a particular family friend's house. I sensed I was strongly and fiercely protected from here on. During those early years of primary school, I was continually told, 'If you don't go to school and be good and learn, child protection services will take you away to a home, because that's what happens to orphans.' And that's what happened to Black kids too. I was terrified and worried about being taken away at school – from my family and town. This still haunts me. My love for school and learning grew quickly and I was good at it, but there was this shadow of fear. A shadow almost like the darkness or the predator of the night would invade my being again.

From that moment in time, I became physically aware of the sensation, just like a light had flicked on inside me. I knew it was my Mother's Spirit waking up to protect her baby. I can remember the exact sensation. I can remember where I was standing and what it felt like. I whispered from a deep inside, place 'It is up to me now; I have to be my protector,' and at that moment an invisible shield formed around me from within, radiating outwards. She was walking within me. I felt her deep sense of wisdom and knowing, and could see through her eyes with much maturity.

I became fiercely independent and began earning my own income and paying taxes when I was 13 years old. Working and studying to secure my future.

Playing basketball and netball became an important part of my growing years. This was when I felt seen, heard and needed, and it gave me a sense of belonging to a team. I guess it seemed like family to me. Between playing these sports, I could be found at the local swimming pool. Swimming and being immersed in water was almost like I was baptizing or purifying myself over and over again. There were times when us kids were banned from the pool, and as teenagers we would sneak to the river at a local hangout spot at the ramp. It didn't seem all that safe though, so we went back to the pool and made things right with Bernie, the manager, and continued swimming there, which just felt safer.

This period of my childhood was the happiest. I love the memories and moments from working and sports that continued through my high-school years. Forming a supportive connection with a certain teacher who walked with me and encouraged that *sense of self-belief* and worth in myself. Feeling a strong sense of being connected and in control. Decades later, acknowledging education and sport saved my life, I have a deep love for them and honour my learning journey. Reflecting on this point of my life is how I saved myself. I did that. I fucking saved myself. I became aware of my own worth and heart with maturity. Being brave and knowing I did not need to be alone or lonely throughout life. Being my own safe place. And that I am not damaged or unwanted. I am sure my Mother's Spirit was guiding me through. All this vital action and these stages in my life moved me safely on to the next milestones that I feel are my biggest lifetime achievements – meeting my life partner and becoming a new mother.

My Mother's Spirit and Gift of Love

The first time I heard 'I love you' was from my husband, Bruce, way back when I was 17 years old. I married him and had his three babies, and I love him endlessly, just as he loves me. It is just a knowing. Just as I knew and felt my Mother's Spirit and love within me. I strongly believe that my mother chose him for me to remind me, teach me and give me a deeper meaning of love. Discovering this in my natal and astrology charts, which depicted our wedding date, made this even more significant to me. And as I research and gaze through old family photos, time and time again, I see more and feel more. There are no orphans in Aboriginal culture and kinship. The tribe looks after you. I look deeply into the photos of my baby portraits, with my mother or father holding me, or being surrounded by the family tribe protecting and watching over me – I was the baby of the family.

And, of course, I am triggered and remember more in the photos of my large extended family – my siblings and cousins were all one. My aunty and sister raised me when my mother died, not long after my father, who had died the year before. Both my aunt and sister had their own children. We were all meshed into one, and there was no separation. We were brothers and sisters. All of us!

> *This should be and can be the definition of love – a deep sense of knowing.*

This is where the conflict rises in me. At times now, looking back, even writing this book, at this moment.

There are many different forms and shapes of love.

I experienced the deepest form and was shaped by the love from my Mother's Spirit; that was enough for me at that young age, at that traumatic time. I did not need to hear it, I guess, all those young years because I felt her. Even though I existed and floated within a big family tribe, I mostly felt I did not belong there. I felt like I was a separate person and often felt alone. I started feeling disconnected from my own being and belonging to anyone.

My explanation for this is that possibly I felt I had to shut myself off to protect myself and not let anyone close to hurt me.

Love is a human need and weaves its way through lifetimes. And what I have learned at age 50 and experienced through life is we need to BE love, breathe love and love ourselves first. Often, we are tricked into assuming that we must look for love elsewhere outside of us, outside our being, and all our energy and effort are consumed in the pursuit of it. I am sure most of us don't really understand love at times or are confused about it as we sit and wait for someone to love us. Just like that damn Tweety-bird!

My life seemed to become a cycle of protection, isolation, disconnection and survival. And through it all, I admit I had forgotten to love myself. There were times a deep darkness invaded within, where my self-love was depleted. There were the lifelong lived experiences and challenges of a deeper ancestral, cultural and spiritual heartache and disconnection of intergenerational trauma being an Aboriginal person in Australia. What is this? Not forgetting lifelong grief and loss and traumatic events.

It is obviously more than a word. And as I reflected on my life and love story and tried to remember when I heard 'I love you' before in my life. I hadn't. Even though I did not hear it, I felt the purest energy of love as a young child growing up in my big family tribe from my Mother's Spirit and during some special moments.

One of those special and most memorable experiences was before the traumatic event, and maybe around the time of being told I was an orphan. It was my birthday. My sister Barb, my guardian at the time, my brother Charlie and my cousins had a big surprise birthday party for me. I remember the lollies, chips and my cousin Phyllis dressing up as a clown to surprise me. I was drawn to a giant bowl of Twisties chips, and hiding inside the bowl were lots of lollipops. I thought I was the luckiest kid. Simple joy and lots of togetherness, connection and happiness. Family. Love. That was the only birthday party I ever really had or remember. Even today. I don't think anything could ever top that. A strong sense of connection, joy, belonging, adventure and hope. Being safe and protected, we were all ONE. I was OK! I was feeling happy and connected, having fun, and I knew I belonged and was part of this big family. I wasn't an 'orphan'! In this, my childhood intact, I lived my own kind of Oneness. We all ate from the same pot of soup on the table each night, and this sustained my large tribe family throughout my childhood. That time was love.

*Today I choose to be love
and weave it through...*

Every moment I breathe.

Every footstep I take.

I am love.

I am love.

I am love.

Once I became a mother, I became fiercely protective, just as my Mother's Spirit was. My life had been filled with trauma, grief and loss. I needed happiness. And I trusted that me and my kids were being watched over. I know this to be so true. My firstborn, Jessica, almost lost her life and continued to fight for it after a tragic accident resulting in a very serious head injury. I slept beside her bed in a country hospital as she was slipping away, and all she wanted was a can of Coke. She was not even two years old. She didn't even drink Coke! I felt she slipped away from me shortly after this request. She was airlifted 500km to the city children's hospital – her father travelling with her. I was still breastfeeding my new baby girl, Emma, so we had to travel by car to the city. This was extremely terrifying as we didn't have mobile phones back then, and I didn't know if she would be alive when I arrived. I was greeted by family members, my sister Emily and brother Phil, who took control, and I felt calmer and in shock at the same time.

A week or so later, I was sitting with my daughter alone in the Intensive Care Unit when the nurses told me they were going to wake her up. She had been in an induced coma since leaving the small country hospital a week earlier. Just as they told me that, they called out her name as I did – calling my baby's name, 'Jessica, baby girl' – and she opened her eyes and looked at me and asked for a can of Coke.

PETUNIAS, EMILY AND HOPE

Petunias can symbolize the desire to never lose hope.

Never lose HOPE.

HOPE has kept me alive for 50 years and more so for the past 30.

My definition of HOPE is Healing, Optimism, Peace, and Empowerment and Education.

This has been my truth, my experience, and I guess I could say my purpose or Dreaming.

The last time I grew petunias was around 30 years ago. I remember being fascinated with them and how long their bloom lasted; the rich pink colours of the flowers as they opened up to the morning sun. My gardening skill at the time was planting in pots. I had three pots of petunias at the back door, facing east, and each morning as I looked at them, with my cuppa, and the rising sun shining on my face, I felt capable, alive and hopeful. My sister Emily was impressed at my gardening skills, my three pots of petunias. She lived close to me, almost next door in fact.

In spring 2021, I was excited and joyful to plant pots and try gardening again. I chose some petunias. A week or so before I turned 50, the petunia seedlings I had planted in three pots at my front door opened up, a rich pink colour, and saluted the morning sun.

At the time I didn't realize how significant this was. I hadn't grown these plants for 30 or so years. I remembered suddenly – while on the phone with my dear friend Meaghan – that there was a huge gap in my memory and gardening efforts, particularly the pots of petunias. They reminded me of my sister Emily. The pink colour reminded me of the bridesmaid dress she wore at my wedding and how she helped me choose a certain shade even from afar; she lived in the big city, six hours' drive away. I grew up being so used to her not being there as she ventured off to the city when I was a young girl. The first time she left me, I remember that I drove with my Aunty Lil to drop her off in the main street to catch the Ansett bus to Melbourne, the capital city, six hours away. She moved that day away from home – the Mallee and Murray River. I cried and cried and cried for days as that bus drove away. I felt broken, scared and alone. I felt like she was my mum, my protector, my favourite person in the world. She did visit at times, and I remember she moved back occasionally. These are the times I loved the most because she became my guardian or carer, and I lived with her at around age eight at a block house surrounded by grapevines. A typical local country environment where the grape vineyards were introduced with the new settlement of the township and gifted to returned soldiers and settlers. Emily even had two black baby goats, which I thought were great. I loved them, my first pets, until they grew and chased me each time I went to the clothesline! Throughout my teenage years, when she lived back home, I stayed with her as much as I could. It was like my heartbeat was in sync with hers, and I needed her the most during those important life milestones.

She was beside me at age 17 when I gave birth to my firstborn, Jessica, and almost two years later when I almost lost Jessica to a traumatic head injury accident and my new little family needed to spend months at the big city children's hospital.

After a few years, she brought her children back home to live and grow with my kids. Our children were almost the same in age at times. Emily even breastfed my second child, Emma, as her own in between feeding her son Daniel. In Aboriginal kinship ways, our babies are one, so they are close like siblings, even today as adults.

I remember the petunias were in bloom when my sister left this world, this lifetime. She died a violent death. I cried, cried, cried until I could not cry out loud any more. Maybe it was the tablets that someone shoved down my throat while I was hysterical after losing my sister hours earlier. I lost all my senses in a single moment that tablet hit my gut. Silently my anger, pain, grief and heartache were trapped, and any happiness, joy and self-love and worth couldn't penetrate. I was numb. I recall the day, just weeks after her death and funeral, sitting at my workplace on the main street and making a strong decision to live. To live for my children and hers, somehow.

Just moments before, I was with the doctor of the time who insisted that my only hope was to take some mood-altering tablets to cope and feel better, to help me get on with life and help me better take care of my three young kids. I angrily refused. It felt similar to the time in primary school when I felt my Mother's Spirit inside me. This, too, was some kind of message from my sister Emily I am sure, almost like she was shielding and protecting me as she always did. It was a very strong 'Fuck that, you're not having that!' I was so angry at the doctor. I chose to live, be safe and be as healthy as I could. No drugs or grog, and to be something, to make a difference, to protect and keep our kids safe. I just didn't know how to at the time. What I knew was that it seemed I sealed the trauma of her death and tried to live around it and not disturb it inside me. That word 'hope' became significant and kept me alive.

Living was my hope.

Thirty years is a long time.

Long time to grow petunias again. The same year as I am writing this very book. And as I am nearing the end of writing and the final chapter, the petunias' lifespan is coming to an end for this season.

Sometimes I am sure it would have been easier to take those tablets, to wipe myself out, to be careless and not responsible, to have no fear, no life, no living, no darkness.

> *'Breathing in the light, the love, the magic, the healing to carry HOPE onwards. The wild wind blows through my hair, bathing me in Grandmother's kisses.'*

I feel like I have written these words and this book a thousand times in my mind, and have been in many lifetimes before. It's already been written by my Ancestors. I am living out my Dreaming and Oneness. I have been writing for the most part of my life in some form and been focused on creating a book and being published. I knew it was important to just start writing. During this time, lots of healing occurred from a very, very deep part of my heart and Soul. The hurt, pain, trauma, sadness and grief. I moved through this with grace and honour and thanked my Higher Self, Soul Spirit and Guides for containing the memories and protecting me.

To have hope was my gift to Self. Hope has saved me over and over again. I was at the time being triggered by life and others around me. Trauma memories were rising and rising, and I had to catch them or reach in to drag these shitty toxic feelings out, like poison killing my life. I wrote, wrote and wrote some more. I loved through it and, importantly, healed through it as the trauma memories were leaving my body for the last time.

Afterwards, I would find childhood photos and remember happiness. My smiling cheeky little face in my school uniform, a photo with my sister Emily – at the river, swimming at Gadsden's Bend – or later in life at a zoo trip with our young babies. I just love how stories and the remembering, good (and bad!), can transform and nurture deep, deep healing. You have to feel to heal. My Soul Spirit feels a deep love each moment I look at my childhood photos and those of my early parenthood. Remembering I was love and my connection to a higher purpose. It gave me a sense of newness, a purity and a clearer connection to my breath.

It was hope. It was living.

•••

I feel now I have broken, unsealed and 'healed' some kind of karmic pattern. To continue living and to simply be alive. To honour others who could not honour themselves. My sister became my hope that kept the light on inside me, leading and guiding the way for me to weave my story and connection back to myself, to my heart, and to home. It's been so fucking tough, though!

> *'Sometimes we forget where home and*
> *sacred space is... it's within us.'*
> **ANNABELLE SHARMAN**

Today I am my own Healer and Medicine. I woke up and remembered the sacred. I became my Dreaming which I now have the words for. I found and became YUMA, the Mutti Mutti language word meaning *BE*.

When I can BE Self, Spirit and Mother Earth, I can Live in Oneness.

Story and writing are now my YUMA healing Medicine and practice.

YUMA is all of the above and, for me, hope. Hope is the 'light that hides in the darkness and waits for that warm flow of energy to take your breath away and resuscitate you back to life'.

Live your truth.

Be brave.

Be love.

Be hope.

*Write your story in a way that heals you,
releases you and loves you.*

Take responsibility and be your own Healer and Medicine.

I needed hope as the guiding light to move through my personal healing. This is my personal experience. As I have written about, almost losing my daughter was a traumatic event that created a path for anxiety to thrive. I became overprotective from that time. I then lost my sister in a most horrific death some short years later. Anxiety flourished, although at the time I did not know its name. I am strongly guided and feel safe writing this part of my story. After losing my sister, I felt much guilt. I was in my early 20s. I was drunk with my friends and family after celebrating a big family event. The guilt built strong, deep, protective walls around my being after this. I didn't hear her. I should have heard her. Why didn't I hear her? I will never get drunk again in this lifetime. Thirty years between growing petunias and carrying guilt and being drunk is a long time. Anxiety found its name in my being shortly after, once I learned and tried to continue through a life of justice and freedom and healing.

Once I had more awareness, 20 years later, I committed to learning new ways to heal and soften the depression and anxiety that has stayed, being comfortable and thriving in my system. I was exploring natural and alternative therapies, which resulted in bringing a deeper level of awareness and understanding about my own mind, body and spiritual and energetic Self. This energy in my body I call 'the darkness', this energy that is and was having an enormous negative effect on my being and consuming me in every way, including my home space environment. There is no other way to describe it but to say it felt, smelled and was seen as a sludge-like mud! A tightly wrapped and knotted ball of darkness that is so tight to unravel, cleanse, visualize or release. At times when I was at home, my body was reacting and being triggered with this instant fear and constant anxiety consuming all the goodness from me, drowning me and sucking the air and breath from me. This feeling settles when my husband is at home or when he walks through the door. Just as when my sister died, I was terrified to be alone at the time. I would avoid being there alone without him. I felt I could fail and not be able to save our son from an epileptic seizure and forget what to do. Being also triggered by my daughter's accident was surfacing more and more. The anxiety became a cycle of control that I didn't realize was so harmful. I do believe, however, that I was being triggered by all this as I was healing from it at the same time. I carried hope, and I know that having hope also saved me and kept me alive in some way.

I no longer feel guilt about my sister's death and will occasionally, on my birthday, have a vodka shot.

MY JOURNEY TO ONENESS

Smoking Ceremony.

My senses are alive, sweet sacred scent of the gum leaves, the Murray River water and red dirt.

Hearing Eagle calling overhead, calling to greet and welcome me home.

The smoke drifting through the trees now looks very mystical and peaceful. The Ancestors are here. I sense them; they are holding me in this magic and sacred moment. I feel their breath, and I now breathe in sync with them. I feel safe and I feel ready.

My Ancestors are dancing and singing me home in this moment, and I feel their breath and heartbeats as the ceremony smoke circles me. I can feel my Mother's and Grandmother's Spirits holding me, protecting me, healing me and leading me back home and back into my body. I can now feel my body. And to be honest, it feels for the first time. I can feel my legs on the ground beneath me – anchoring and grounding me. My breath rises and falls in and out, in and out. My eyes are closed but now I can see.

*In Oneness, we dance together to the rhythm
of the gentle breath. Together we stoke the fire
energy of Ancestors as we reconnect back into our
bodies and back into our spiritual soundness.*

We be in breath.

*We be in the stillness of our body, in the quiet, in the
calm, and deep down into the centre of our soulfulness.*

I open my eyes, and the smoke gently floats around me and the flame – for the fire is gently easing. I cannot seem to take my eyes off the flames. I sit on Mother Earth now, and the profound feelings reach my inner being to the core. I feel a presence next to me and a gentle hand on my shoulder; it is my friend Sissy by my side. We sit in silence for a little while, and again the Eagle flies over us and across the river.

After this life-changing and profound cultural, spiritual event – my first Smoking Ceremony – I initially felt a little lost or unsure.

Although this feeling didn't last too long, and I soon became more confident in my healing and moved forward into the future with a deep strength that seemed to be activated that day.

After further reflection, I came to understand my healing more and more. This sensation of feeling my body for the first time scared me. But now I know it happened so I can feel my body without all the layers. I had been stripped bare of all the pain, grief and worry which I had carried for far too long – even more so since my sister's death. And I am comfortable to say now that I have used these things as protection and became friendly with them. I silently bathed in the glory of pain and suffering, the guilt and shame, and held on to my lost loved ones assuming I was living and creating their legacy – living life to the fullest, providing a great life for my family, doing wonderful and successful work for my community and saving others. All the while hiding from myself, dying of numbness. I was *Waking Up*.

I now just needed to take one footstep at a time and honour my life and history without it controlling and suffocating me, and rolling me through life bump after hard bump. My new focus was to live in a healthier way. I became a bit excited and visioned for the first time, a life healing my trauma story. However, I knew there was maybe a new big lesson and practice I had to step into to reach that healing, and that was forgiveness.

*I breathe and dance with my Ancestors
when I close my eyes and Dream...*

*They guide me to create the Rhythm
of Light to HEAL Mother Earth,
my people and humanity.*

Healing Hands, Healing Spirit

Many years ago, I was at a great pause and felt like I was drowning and suffocating, working in and for the system as a social and community worker. One that didn't respond well to a strong Black woman in a male-dominated and -managed organization. Not being valued, respected or celebrated for your skills, qualifications and integrity can be (and was for me) a very harmful experience. Being pushed to the brink of burnout and then exploding and quitting, resulting in me leaving damaging workplaces. I did nothing but recover and continue my healing journey.

One sunny day I am feeling very positive and was calling Spirit to guide me and show me the ways. 'What am I going to do next?' I asked. I was reading the local I newspaper at the time and turned the page, and an advertisement appeared to blink and call me in. The advert read 'Learn about your chakras.' I thought, *What is that?!* I had no idea but was intrigued, and the idea of it all seemed to talk and connect with my heart and Soul.

I called the number and said my name, 'Annabelle Sharman'. The lady on the other end hangs up the phone. I thought, *Oh*, and I called again. This time I said, 'I am needing more information about the chakra workshop.' The lady said, 'Did you just call?' I said, 'Yes'. She hangs up again.

I was a little bit pissed off at this stage and so I called again – third time lucky, right? The same lady answered and once again I said what I said before and she said, 'Is Sharman your real name?' I said, 'Yes. My name is Annabelle Sharman. I live in Robinvale and I want to come to your workshop.' She went silent for a moment and I was actually feeling really annoyed now. She said to me, 'Is it really your name?' Again, I said 'YES.' So, I enrolled and travelled up the highway to the nearby town to do this workshop.

Oh, how interesting this workshop was! Who would have thought that this is what our energy centres are called and they have colours? But I totally got it; it all made sense to me. I thought, *Maybe this is where I will learn about my throat issues.* 'Chakras' is not a word that is familiar to me or part of my language. I remembered some of the other ladies present talking about Reiki – having it and learning it. I could feel my Spirit rise like an antenna, and I was so, so intrigued that by the time I drove the hour trip home, I had booked in for a Reiki session.

I was becoming excited and nervous as I went along to my session. Although I was unsure of the process, I knew I was totally guided here and fully open to receiving what was coming. There were even crystals!

An hour or so later I couldn't feel my body but could feel it all at the same time. I cried and felt like by the time my feet touched the ground off that healing table I was stepping into a new being – body. I felt my heartbeat again. A healed being – heart, mind and body. I was calm and grounded. *Oh my fucking God!* I thought out loud and whispered to my Soul. I had been having counselling therapy and seeing a psychologist for my grief and trauma for 10 years, and in one hour it was all gone. It is my actual truth and healing experience. Funnily enough, I haven't had any throat issues since that day. Now I am a Social Worker and a Counsellor and I work in mental health. Spirit and the Ancestors led me here and found me just as I found myself touching my feet on the ground getting off the table.

From this moment in time, my whole world changed and obviously, from here, I deeply reflected how I could take that energy to help heal my community and others in need. So, this became my new direction. Unemployed and loving it at the time made space for me to create, and I quickly began learning, training, and becoming an energy healing practitioner. With a focus on how to heal trauma. Learning as much as I could and needed.

I journeyed and became a Reiki Master teacher, learning about Crystal Therapy and Emotional Freedom Techniques (EFT).

A swarm of bees visited the location the day I received my Reiki certificate. It seemed, or I could feel, they came to greet and celebrate my Soul. It reassured me of the honouring of a new life I would lead from here on. I have since been told, 'The bee totem is a helpful symbol for manifesting things the bee symbolizes, including fertility, health and vitality, and prosperity. It's also a good luck totem for being productive in your work and finding work that is fulfilling.'

I continued learning and developing a holistic healing business, along with going back to part-time work in the family violence sector, which surprised me greatly. I honour my teachers for stepping into my life energy and journey at the time I needed them most, and I deeply thank my Ancestors and my teachers' Ancestors. I was learning and healing all at the same time, teaching and my own healing in synchronicity, it seems. Something very transformational was happening here, and I gained a new breath and energy for life and – for once – in a very long time, I was enjoying my work and career and especially creating my new holistic healing business.

The Ochre Dance

I danced in the rhythm of the beat and sound of the clapsticks, moving the ochre with my feet and through my hands. Feeling Mother and Ancestors dancing with me. Over the coming months I was joined by my daughter and friend Sistah, and we all danced together in sync and creation. Preparing a sacred space to gather, this special, special space, a healing space. A place to nurture me while returning home.

I was certain that my brother, Charlie, who had passed over in the Dreamtime just months before, had guided me to this space to heal and hold my grief. You see, most of my siblings are great Artists, including him, creating paintings, jewellery and traditional woodcraft instruments. During my brother's final living week, he somehow reunited and gathered my family to sit and just Be with him in my sister Barb's art shed, which is known as the 'Shed'. We sat while he painted his final painting and drew on his final green smoko, cups of tea, laughs, tears and waking hours. It was a week-long ceremony of love and honour. I experienced the biggest lesson, that of forgiveness, during this grieving, healing time.

Sitting in stillness with him alone in his hospital room, I felt hopeless and was unsure how I could be helpful. At this stage he could not eat, and he just wanted a final meal of curry chicken, so off I went to ceremonially create this pot of curry with all the love I had in me. He was unable to eat it, but he was able to experience the taste on his tongue and the smell.

Through the following days, his final days, I ensured Bob Marley and The Rolling Stones were playing. The simplicity. A sacred honouring and holding space for his pass over.

This experience woke me up more and more. I am very familiar with death and have experienced most of my siblings dying throughout my life – almost always in tragic, traumatic circumstances. Being present often with the family tribe while loved ones were taking their last breath on this Earth. Also, my parents passing while I was a toddler maybe prepared me for this lifelong journey of death. It almost became a normal and expected event that we experienced together and regularly. This particular experience taught me and reminded me of a deep, deep love of family – a sacred love. Reflecting now back to that time, it was as though my brother already was an angel. I felt as though the Soul Spirit of our parents, grandparents and siblings, and generations of Ancestors, were him. Bringing us all in and waking us all up and healing us in a way we did not realize at the time.

The following months my Spirit felt called to return over and over again to the Shed. Needing and feeling the need to be creative. Now, I do not call myself an Artist in any way, not like most of my siblings. I painted over the coming months, creating this amazing floor mural at the Shed. I painted in ceremony, honour and hope. I did not know the title of the painting at that delicate time. But it was a deep knowing. I was living and breathing this painting, each day, over and over again, in a trance-like state. Painting through hot summer days and nights in mostly 40-degree heat. I could feel it healing me each time I picked up that brush and created new colours. Blessing me, cleansing me and loving me with every stroke of the brush.

Once it was complete, I sat during a hot summer evening with my new dear friend, Jenny. We sat and were mesmerized. I had not long met her at a Crystal Therapy workshop, and she kept connecting and visiting me, so I guess I made an impression and deep connection with her. Or, importantly, our Souls did. While we both sat and stared at this great mural art piece on the floor, I asked her with curiosity what she meant by 'Shaman'. It was not a word I was familiar with, but it was my married surname. Listening to her reply, the title of the floor mural suddenly came into being – *Journey to Oneness*. I used this space for a year or so after, being creative and offering healing gatherings with other women in the community. The space was alive with energy, Spirit and healing. When you walked on the floor, you could feel the vibrations from it. Sometimes when I was there alone, it felt and looked like the floor was dancing. Bringing a sudden sense of calm and peace.

A short time after, I found a piece of my brother Charlie's painting, and was guided to look up at my sister Emily's framed jewellery piece that hangs on my lounge room wall. I could not believe it when the two pieces were side by side or overlaid; it looked like a representation of the floor mural *Journey to Oneness* I just painted earlier. I sensed their Spirits were with me during that Creation time. This blew my mind and gave me a stronger sense of Spirit and belief.

On reflection of this time of my journey, my creativity was activated in a big way. Wanting to use my healing hands to paint and draw with ochre, paperbark and healing plants, feathers, quandong seeds and crystals. I was deeply connecting culturally and spiritually and being more and more grounded and healed in so many ways. I was hungry to learn more and explore deep in the bush with my friend Sistah. We went on many, many bush adventures caring for the country, and collecting and gathering for ceremony. And we still do. To just Be and be still and breathe with Mother (Earth). To be in a pure space in the middle of the bush with my bare feet on the ground was what I craved and needed. It woke me up. I felt at one with my Ancestors.

Being creative is healing me in ways that also connect and ground me spiritually and culturally.

At times my brothers' Spirits walk with me and beside me in the bush in my dreams. During the time creating the special sacred healing space, my other brother Noel's Spirit visited my dream and walked with me in one of those bush walks. He was having a great yarn and told me, 'Sista, you need these stones,' showing me three distinct stones in his hands. They were crystals. Earlier that very year, I discovered a great crystal shop in the nearby town which became a significant space for support and healing and, of course, crystals. My brother Noel lived in the big city away from me growing up, and I didn't see him often, but he was there for me when I needed him the most, even though he was in Spirit.

Why Forgiveness?

I wrote earlier about practising forgiveness. This is where my Ancestors and Spirit are strongly guiding me to write this, so I will make no apologies here. This is my story. What this means for me is: Forgiveness can become a dirty word!

I Just Want To Be Black. However, at times it feels as though I am not Black enough or too Black; it hurts. This country and its system continue to oppress and shun my Blackness. I just say this outright: in my opinion, Australia is the most racist country in the world to its First Nations peoples – Aboriginal people. I know as I live through it, and generations upon generations before me knew it. While I was studying for my Social Work degree and completing my work placement at the local hospital, my Social Work supervisor told me that I could not attend or accompany her to home visits because the residents were racists. Once I graduated and took on positions, systemically I was given only Black clients. This happened to me continuously in mainstream roles throughout my career.

I was always the only Black person in the room. A Black dot in a white world, a world that supported the vanishing and removal of that Black dot, my people Aboriginal people. How do and can we live, navigate, stay safe, feel safe, be culture, be Black?

How can we forget and forgive? Forgiveness is reachable, is possible. But when a system is white and continues control through generations upon generations, forgiveness becomes a dirty word. How can peace and freedom ever be experienced in this country? This lucky country! We just want to be Black. Be the Dreaming of generations of grandmothers before us. We are not dogs, savages, freeloaders, no-hopers, dolebludgers. We don't need saving. We are heroes, warriors, survivors, the Dreamers. We are Creation. We are Mother Earth. We are the land, water, air, fire, Spirit. When you continually wipe your dirty feet on Her, on us, the mark and stain remains and deepens; it becomes fused in history. A history of shame, hate and mistrust. A history of unsafeness. A history without hope that sounds like oppression.

My Spirit will always grieve the fact that our land has been taken. Daily I, we, grieve for the land! When the new township was built in my hometown, the soil – Earth – was removed from what my people call the 'Sandpit' to build footpaths and roads. Every truckload of earth removed contained Ancestral remains of my people, the Aboriginal people. You see, the Sandpit is a Significant and Cultural Burial Ground, where I imagined many gatherings and ceremonies happened and possibly battles were fought. But importantly, it was the final resting place for generations of Ancestors. I have heard many non-Aboriginal people say and assume that it happens everywhere else. Well, it happened here on this land, on our riverbanks and waterways, on the grapevines in this town, on your paddocks, and most likely on every new township, traditional country and boundary you walk upon in this country, Australia, worldwide and Mother Earth. These events and activities have never and most likely will never be acknowledged or written officially as truth in the white council and historical pages.

> *Every day the paths and roads are walked*
> *and driven on. My Ancestors feel it.*

I teach and tell this truth and many more to my children and grandchildren, just as my sister and Elders did to me. We must teach all our children that the Earth, soils and waters are our Ancestors, and we are One and we are the same. We must protect Mother and all she contains. Acknowledge and respect her from a deep part of your Soul, heart and Spirit. Be One with her just as I teach and share YUMA – to BE Self, Spirit and Mother Earth.

> *Be gentle with your footsteps*
> *For our Ancestors need to rest;*
> *They feel your intention,*
> *Walk gentle with your breath.*

So, there's that; even before I was born and dreamed into this colonized world and country!

I come to accept and honour my parents for giving me life whilst they were reaching 50 years of age and living in a time when the

Assimilation policy was being enforced on Aboriginal people, even in my little country community. I am the 10th child. The final child, the miracle baby, the peacekeeper who will rise up and change the world. Once I believed this, and trusted and culturally and spiritually connected further within, I became that energy. The energy of the *Spirit Weaver*.

As an Aboriginal person, I follow a different map. *Our unique map ensures the Songlines and Dreaming remain intact and are honoured and practised, seen, heard, sung, danced and healed.* The typical map of Australia is a colonized map and has no relevance to me.

> *It is the unfurling of fear and conditioning and the recoiling of love, Ancestors, heart, Soul and YUMA.*
>
> *It is the korus bringing new life and purity to each and every one of us. It is the peace, tranquillity and spirituality that is at One. It is the strength of new beginnings.*

Forgiveness feels so hard to reach when there has been violence, abuse and mistreatment. As a dedication to my early childhood trauma and my sister Emily who, as I mentioned, died violently, I chose to live to stay alive and to grow and protect my kids and be healthy. For me to do this, I had to somehow forgive. To forgive the people who could not protect me as an innocent little girl. Forgive myself for being drunk. Forgive her for leaving me. I will never completely forgive the man who took her life. My energy needed to change, so I could not focus on 'the man'. I released myself so I could live and heal.

Many, many years later, after I was healing and learning and becoming whole again, and when I was strong enough spiritually and culturally, my sister's Spirit came to me. I was awake and healed and I was ready. I know she is always with us, and watches over her two new granddaughters, and I wait for the day they, the babies, can travel home on country here to the Murray River for their welcome and blessing ceremony. Where their grandmother Emily's Spirit can ceremony with them among the gum trees on the riverbank.

Living a life of needing to be safe, culturally safe, spiritually safe, emotionally safe, I will never apologize for, and I will continue to strive to ensure the people I work with have this sense of safety that is needed. As mentioned earlier, I began working and healing in the family violence sector, and I feel I was able to provide a safe, gentle place for women and children to land, connect, rest, breathe and heal. I feel this is the best of me and my work, and whichever sector I choose to journey through in my career in the future, I will ensure it be a safe space.

SPIRIT WEAVER

Breathing the same breath as my Ancestors is my centre, my home, heart, Soul. Is Oneness.

*I am Warungan Mayi: 'Living Spirit
of an Aboriginal Being'.*

*My dearest lifelong friend, Sistah, blessed
me and reminded me with this name.*

*Warungan Mayi – I am a living Spirit
of an Aboriginal Being.*

*I choose to honour every breath and
footstep to live in Oneness.*

*Walking Spirit and embodying my purpose of
Healing is the call or wish of my Ancestors.*

The Spirit Weaver has woken up.

The Spirit Weaver, for me, is an energy, and this energy invited me and offered a lifeline to healing that was needed deeply. I chose healing, I accepted the invitation. I have embodied the Spirit Weaver energy and will continue to empower others on their healing journeys.

As I age and write this book, I become more awake and aware of traditional cultural and spiritual practices. As a grandmother of three grandsons and stepping into an Eldership, I am guided and discover more and more details of my Ancestral lineage and the thread that connects me to the land and the waterways.

I feel drawn deeply to these waterways, especially the Murray River. I was born and continue to live in a small rural town surrounded by the Murray. I sit often and watch the water ripple and shimmer when the morning sun's rays touch it gently. I am proud to say I am a Bush River woman, and that is where you will find me most often, mainly on the banks of the river or deep in the bush among the gum trees. It is beautiful, and in these moments, I feel as though this waterway and these trees are sharing deep ancestral knowledge and wisdom with me. It is just a knowing.

Energy flowing
Light moving through the water

Waves are harmonizing the energy flow

That sings to my heart and Soul Spirit.

A remembering.

A Knowing.

Growing up, I was told by my family Elders that we take our mother's tribe. And the knowledge at the time was the Mutti Mutti tribe, and later in life, after research and learned cultural connection and kinship, further strong lineages to the nearby Nari Nari tribe. This will be my new journey to explore and plant my footsteps on this land, which are my Ancestral Homelands here in Australia. And I know in my future, I will eventually make way over the waterways to my father and grandfather's homeland of New Zealand, to which I have had a calling over the past years now.

In Australia it can be difficult to follow the Dreaming or Songlines if they have been broken. Meaning the language, land, waterways, ceremony, way of life, cultural, spiritual and being has been systemically taken by a colonized government. I feel in my Spirit a connection to both tribes, as my grandmother has shown me in real life as a little girl and in my dreams. She is calling me home to country. I know this so deeply as I travel and step onto the soil, land, water of the area. I feel her hold me. I know I belong. I know

I am home. It is a beautiful feeling when you have a deep sense of connection. I explain it as breathing the same breath in sync with my grandmother and Ancestors.

Mystical peppercorn trees sit silently and at peace on the foreshore, home to many creatures.

Energy flowing, light moving through the lake.

Waves harmonizing the energy flow that sings to my heart.

It becomes an orchestra of life and synchronicity.

Standing strong feet on the ground. I feel connected as though I was with my grandmother when she was born on this land.

The grand gatekeeper tree draws my attention, the gentle movement in the nest atop. A newborn chick's ruffled feathers pop up over the sides of his nest.

New life, new energy.

The hope for humanity brings feeling and gratitude to my heart, then to my Soul.

My grandmother speaks to me through the shimmering waves, bathing me, blessing me, initiating me in her wisdom, faith and breath.

Removing doubts, pain, injustices.

Breathing in the light, the love, the magic,
the healing to carry HOPE onwards.

The wild wind blows through my hair, bathing me in
Grandmother's kisses. I then feel the winds circling me as
though they are a million more kisses from my Ancestors.

My Dreaming.

Cleansing, renewing and regenerating life, humanity.

While I was there on traditional country, she held me, and when I needed it most, I felt her carry me. I knew she was breathing with me.

I embodied all the elements and will later learn the significance.

I celebrate her, my grandmother, and I now know my Dreaming is to *live in Oneness* every day, in every breath and in every way. To just Be. My life represents Oneness. I live Self, Spirit and Mother Earth. Through story, actions, healing, being, sharing, caring, loving, breathing and telling the stories that need to be told. To become your own Healer and Medicine. Honouring my mother and grandmother's strong Spirit connection and knowing guided me to *YUMA*, meaning *BE*. A Mutti Mutti language word.

In this lifetime, I am, or I have become, the Spirit Weaver, living Self, Spirit and Mother Earth. I have become the Master of my own healing journey, having learned my own lessons through life. I am a survivor, and now I am Home, am whole and I am Oneness. As the Spirit Weaver, my Dreaming is to journey, connect, heal and bring people back home to their own Self, Spirit, heart and breath with grace, honour and peace so they may feel and experience Oneness. Weaving those broken threads of ancestral knowledge, knowing and wisdom back together.

As I have now celebrated 50 years Earthside, I feel like my light has been turned back on or is shining even brighter now. Previous days and weeks before that milestone, I was feeling very distressed with the state of the country and even in my state and region. The uncertainty, the lack of hope, the loss of control, choice and freedoms. The morning of the big birth date, I was woken up by my father's Spirit. I have not been witness to him before now. He waited for me to turn this powerful age to embrace me, to wake me up when I needed it most to save myself. I saw and felt his strong dark hands reach in and hold me. I heard him tell me: 'Get up! No one is going to rescue you.' In that moment, I woke up. I feel so loved and alive, with a strength to fight for freedom, to stand for freedom and to be freedom as a Future Ancestor.

Reflecting and knowing, I was always determined to be free and not trapped in the system of my earlier childhood story of being an orphan and the real threat of being taken away from my tribe. My mother's words and gift back then at that tender age were a similar experience to my mother's Spirit – I was to be my own protector, it's just me. I felt her Spirit enter my body, and felt I saw through her mature experienced eyes during my teenage and early adult years.

My power was my education; it saved me, or I saved myself through education. As I mentioned earlier, I also worked from the age of 13, earning my own income and being fiercely and proudly independent, working at the hairdressers that still exists today and whose owner, Pauline, has become a lifelong friend. I graced that establishment until I was about to become a young mother myself at the age of 17. Jessica, my firstborn, followed by Emma and then my only son, Zachary. I worked damn hard, learning and studying Social Work full-time, and beginning an extensive career and paying my taxes here in Australia. I lived my life while my mother's protective Spirit embraced me, determined to stay out of the system, not to have my kids taken away from me, or to be controlled or oppressed or a statistic – that caused so much damage to my Ancestors and just generations before me. Even now, today, that systemic intergenerational trauma exists widely. It's called 'colonization'.

Later in life, brave enough and over many years, I developed my own business – creating my own healing ways and practice offering YUMA Healing. Throughout my working life experiences, I have had the privilege to witness, hear and honour many stories. The history and stories from my people, Aboriginal people of Australia, have often been poisoned and tarnished with mistruths, hate and dishonour. And many times, the stories have never been told, or my people written about with the respect, justice and honour they deserve. This is why there are two different stories being told in Australia, this lucky country of ours.

Today, I believe our Ancestors are connecting and guiding us together to share their breath, join the dots, and these moments allow people to be **heard, held and healed**. *In those moments, I become the Spirit Weaver.* The ability to hold space and time, to protect and nurture the flow of history and Dreaming. Weave the truth, love and meaning. Guide that pure energy and light to bless through your story and healing.

I feel I have been there before! Been here before.

Dancing with the darkness. With the shame. With the pain and fear. Finding ways to heal through my trauma story and those before me. This feels like a new way to heal my People, all people. But I am sure it is the old way. The original way. The natural way.

To Be Oneness and Be Self, Spirit and Mother Earth. To bring the stories to life and truth-telling. Stepping into the light or holding that torch high and proud to illuminate the path for those who follow us. As the Spirit Weaver, I encourage all to return home, to Mother Earth, to Oneness.

Current situation in the big system of this so-called free country, the day I turned 50 years of age I was officially 'unemployable' for the first time in my life. I see it as being released, and I accept that with honour and pride. Although events today remind me of a 'new colonization' here in Australia, this lucky country. Way back then, there was a fear of Blacks; it's now a fear of the unvaccinated, diminishing human rights and choice. There's much displacement, separation, privilege, hate and trauma. As I write, citizens need a certificate or permit to travel and live freely in and through boundaries and states. Sounds very familiar. Look deeper, and research will lead you to early colonization in Australia and government policies at play that set a path of destruction and alienation, dissolution and, to be frank, to wipe out my people – the first people of this country.

Today I remind myself through the darkness and anxious moments when I worry for my three grandsons' future: We are free. I am free. Ancestors fought hard for us all. I am proud of who I have become.

We are all Future Ancestors.

I will rise.

We can rise together.

I will meet you there.

Our light is bright.

*Each day we can walk to
the Rhythm of Oneness.*

I am not proud of this system and country in which I live. Its history and new history is shameful. I write this because the story needs to be told. The truth needs to be revealed. And as a time capsule, one day, my future grandchildren may read this. This Warrior woman of Phyllis and Frank and granddaughter of Emily is here and is free and is writing this story. Today she is the Spirit Weaver, and she will continue to sit along the Murray River, catching the morning sunrise daily, a place her parents enjoyed just being when they were with her.

Weave the truth.

Weave the story.

Weave your way home.

Oneness is a way of being that transcends the mind and physical plains.

In Oneness, we are connected with everything in existence.

We are one.

It is fullness, infinite expansion and wholeness.

It is the unfurling of fear and conditioning and the recoiling of love, Ancestors, heart, Soul and YUMA.

*It is the korus bringing new life and purity
to each and every one of us.*

*It is the peace, tranquillity and spirituality that is
at One. It is the strength of new beginnings.*

It is our personal growth, positive change and awakening.

It is our perpetual movement around the edges.

It is our interwoven selves in the stars of the Ancestors.

The threading together of Spirit, earth and body.

Our breath.

Our stillness.

And all in one breath, we are One.

We are everything and we are nothing but Oneness.

YUMA

WISDOM WHISPERS

Be Self

We be in breath.

*We be in the stillness of our body, in the quiet, in the
calm and deep down into the centre of our soulfulness.*

*Come a little closer, feel your breath,
hear your breath. That is you.*

*When you are searching outside of you, in the lonely,
through the sadness, the grief and the unknown.*

Come back.

Just look down.

Just look down.

*Find your feet; you are standing here,
you are alive, you are Self.*

Move through your body, feel your breath. Feel your heartbeat.

You are the universe, the Ancestors.

Your story.

You are all of that and more than you know.

Be Self.

BE in the stillness of Self.

As I was writing this book and reflecting on my process, I told myself that I would tell others: make sure you write from a place of love if you are going to write a book or your story. My earlier writings were from a place of deep, dark, silent trauma, and it depleted and truly exhausted me, and I felt empty. I felt like I was continually telling this trauma narrative – like a joyous merry-go-round ride, and I was enjoying the ride over and over again because that's all I knew – on repeat.

However, I now know that was necessary. Moving through the cycle of all this trauma allowed me to jump off at the end of the ride, being healed. Feeling healed and feeling heard and free. It doesn't matter where you start. Just start with your breath, find your feet and feel your heartbeat. Love will show up. You will hear your voice and your story and feel in your body once again, or maybe for the first time. Trust comes from within, and you have to BE Self to fully own your story and healing.

This is me being love and being Self writing this book, *The Future Ancestor*, the ride of my life.

'It is fullness, infinite expansion and wholeness.'

PART TWO

Ceremony

This section is made up of the following chapters in which I will share stories and teachings that will connect you, the reader, to the Earth and your Ancestors.

- Gathering Gum Leaves

- Elements

- Pot of Soup

- Just Add Water

- Light the Flame

- Air – Wind

- The Rise

Ceremony feels like moving in sync with the vibrations of your heartbeat, the beat of the drum – or tapping clapsticks in my Aboriginal culture. Living in sync with the Elements and Mother Earth, gathering the leaves and wood for the sacred fire, lighting the flame, sprinkling the Murray water over the leaves and then breathing in the scent of the Eucalyptus gum leaves in a smoking ritual, to BE in direct connection with Ancestors in that moment. To feel hope and listen to and hear the Grandmother's wisdom whispers – for me, a strong cultural Aboriginal woman, I call this 'YUMA', a Mutti Mutti language word meaning '*BE*'.

This chapter will reflect on my journey to Oneness and the introduction of **YUMA** as the **Healing and Being Practice**. As a Future Ancestor to all the Future Ancestors reading this book, I will share the Ancestral wisdom whispers in ways that will encourage and empower us to be our own Healer and Medicine.

I breathe with my Ancestors
when I close my eyes and dream.

They guide me to create the Rhythm of Light to
heal Mother Earth, My People and Humanity.

GATHERING GUM LEAVES

I am welcomed and embraced into a private healing blessing ceremony. I knew this was going to be a profound life-changing event. I was summoned by my father's Spirit and his people, with the ancient ones of this land. I felt like I was in a dream. It was time for me to step into my Dreaming, and it was time for me to follow my healing path and purpose.

The candles were glowing, and the warm energy was vibrating and dancing in the room. I felt it the moment I arrived in my car. It was like a surge of warm energy wrapped tightly and nurturing its way around me, as though my Ancestors were all holding me at the same time. I felt nervous at what was about to happen.

As I sat in the comfy chair, I felt that others were present in the room. I felt the energy; it felt electric. I felt love and I felt safe. I breathed deeply in that moment. I was told they were breathing in sync with me. We were all breathing the same breath. There was a ceremony about to commence. The Ancient ones of my people appeared very, very ancient – a female and a male tribal Elder. They were there to present me the healing gifts to take into the future. I received in ceremony a sacred smoking followed by a coolamon with water and a coolamon of gum leaves. *'You have permission. Create and weave the wisdom and Medicine.'* I was then culturally attuned to higher vibration through my energy centres, one by one, and given instructions of the lands I need to touch – the Earth and across the ocean – for further alignment. I could not believe this was happening.

How did they know I was here; I was waiting; I was ready? The Māori Healer was just as mystified and moved as I was, and she, too, received a blessing of gratitude.

I was given visions of Cloths, gum leaves and water. The Cloths were gracefully folded in bundles, and there were piles upon piles of them. This is when I clearly realized that this is my Healing Creation, *the Spirit Cloths* that I had created for ceremonial purposes just a little while earlier for a local group of women for the Repatriation of Ancestral Remains ceremony. I will talk more about the significance of this Repatriation further along in this story.

It all made deep sense to me now. The gum leaves and the Murray River water were my Medicine to alchemize for healing. It seems so simple. As it should be, I believe.

After this very special and deeply healing experience, I became more and more aware of where I was locating myself, towards the riverbanks to gaze in silence at the ripples of the water and being among the gum trees in the bush. Oh, this was my paradise, and this was quickly my daily practice. Have you ever smelled a eucalyptus gum leaf? If you have not, I want you to.

When I hold a gum leaf in my hand, I am at one with the leaf, the tree and the Mother from which it was grown. The water that runs deep through the roots. Just as I am in Ancestral Spirit, the majestic Ancient Tree. The wisdom keeper that's deeply rooted and rises and shines as high as the sun and spreads far and wide to protect and nurture, feed and support and hold space for many, many others. As I have learned along the way while creating the Spirit Cloths and then as they travel to their new owners and I hear stories of gratitude once they arrive.

The Spirit Cloth is a very powerful conduit, just like a transdermal effect. This word 'transdermal' I am not familiar with, but this word came clearly through the night from my Ancestors for me to tell the story of the Spirit Cloth. Once the Cloth reaches its being or owner, it has an effect that can sometimes be indescribable. But the experience and feeling are almost immediate. Personally, I wrap and use the Spirit Cloth when my knee pain throbs through the night – it's an instant pain relief – or when I am overwhelmed and my anxiety is raging.

The Cloths offer instant calm, balance, ease, love and connection for many. They have wrapped newborn babies and individuals at their end of life. There are hundreds of stories of the Spirit Cloth. This YUMA effect is a healing way of Being through the Spirit Cloth.

> *You, found in the tree that held you, in the*
> *strength of your Ancestors' arms.*

I was in awe that I was gifted by the Ancient ones this plant of life, plant of healing, that is so plentiful and abundant. There are about 900 species in the three genera eucalyptus, corymbia and angophora. Almost all eucalypt species are native to Australia. Eucalypts evolved from rainforest Ancestors, adapting to an environment in which drought, nutrient-poor soils and fire were increasingly common. These plants evolved and adapted and are resilient, just like the Aboriginal people of this country. Survivors.

The gum leaves are used widely and freely by Aboriginal people for cultural smoking ceremony practices and have been since the beginning of time. And I was about to embark and develop a deeper connection and understanding of its powerful Medicine for healing.

In saying this, the more I became aware, it was almost as if I became the tree. When going on holidays and travelling, I am fascinated and greet the trees as if they are my family. My senses search for some leaves at specific times and places. The trees and leaves are my meaning, and I will often pull the car over and sit quietly and breathe in the scent and be at One.

On one special occasion recently I was visiting Manatunga Mission, which is a very sacred place to my local Aboriginal community. I was standing on the spot of the original mission house where my grandmother Emily lived. She was a great gardener, I have been told. While moving around the area, being very aware of my footsteps, I noticed a small plant. I looked deeply for a minute and realized it was a particular gum leaf that is not that usual for the area. Carefully I walked towards it, my heart beating with excitement. And there it was, three new plants all huddled together. I picked a leaf to have a smell. And suddenly, I was transported; it was the purest scented gum I had smelled. It was more than a smell; it was a sacred gift I smelled the night of the sacred ceremony spoken of earlier. While I smelled it, I imagined my mother and grandmother there beside me and being in ancient times in the bush with them and surrounded by all the Ancestors. It was a feeling that I cannot fully describe, but the closest would be a sense of pure bliss and sacredness. This moment and experience was healing for me.

As I move through this new healing awareness I discover more and experiment more with the Spirit Cloth and the healing this has created for many.

My Journey and Medicine with the Spirit Cloth

As I mentioned earlier, several years ago, at a very vulnerable healing time, I received my very first Ceremonial Smoking along the Murray River, where my parents, grandparents and Ancestors lived. This was a very profound healing experience and remembering. I was encouraged and inspired to continue and feel a deep connection to Mother Earth, my Spirit and Self. The gum leaf plays a big part of this new healing way. I continually visioned how I could take that memory, experience and connection to Mother Earth with me everywhere during those healing times when I felt I needed a 'big energetic healing hug'.

I experimented firstly with making Spirit Cloths for my Healing Room and Spaces, and I then made others for a special group of women with intentions for protection and healing during a time

When all the elements combine

It is a perfect balance of all there is

And with this balance

It is the Oneness

It is harmony

And in this,

Not forgetting the human element

Our human Spirit

The thread that alchemizes all

*The elements to share
in nature's beauty.*

of Repatriating Ancestral Remains along the Murray River. The Cloths were like a cloak of armour but of blessings and honour. I slept with mine and wrapped myself in it while on country, energetically preparing that land for the return ceremony.

The wind raged and ripples flowed fiercely through the water in the days leading up to the ceremony. We camped on site and watched and waited in silence for the day to arrive. We watched as the waves lapped the riverbank, and all the undercurrents from every direction seemed to travel in the one direction to the edge of the cliff where the Remains would be returned. As the day came closer, the intensity of the waves, wind and water grew. I have permission from my Elders to write about this here.

There is something like no other, holding up to 11,000-year-old Ancestral Remains of your people in your hands to rebury and return them to Mother Earth after they had been in boxes in private collections and museums for 30 years, having been stolen from the original resting places in this country. The women-only group gathered, young and old, all moving in sync and silence, honouring and celebrating and having a deep sense we were returning justice and balance and healing for the higher good. We cried and cried and finally, silently, sang our Ancestors back home.

I experienced this with my daughter and grandsons; this is one of the most profound healing events we could have practised and it will remain with us always. Through the evening and night, there was a welcome calmness of the Elements as if balance had been restored, and we continued to sit around the campfire – feeling in awe, emotional, healed and justified. This place and land, we will continue to travel and protect the space and have ceremony and sit by the riverbank and smell the gum leaves. I will continue to do that while walking this human life and in the Dreamtime.

Since this time, I have continued to create my Spirit Cloths during full moons and with the golden ingredients of the gum leaves and the Murray River, and the infusion of the healing energy of Reiki, love, intention and ceremony.

ELEMENTS

As my footsteps go further into the bush, I feel my emotions rise and I close my eyes. I hear the rhythm flow through me. I am swaying in sync to the beat only I can hear. My feet move and step and dance in ceremony. The ancient sacred Ancestors' voices echo through my being and then through the gum trees that line the riverbank.

As I am standing here, I connect to my future generations of grandchildren.

I hear them saying my name, I see them being YUMA, I feel their breath, and I breathe and dance with them. I am a breath in their Dreamings.

My heart beats for them, creating a ripple and vibration that will land and remain in this sacred part of Mother. I will always be here, just as my Ancestors are here with me now, as though I was standing high on the threshold, waiting to move into a newness, a beginning, a becoming.

I have arrived.

I am here.

Can you hear me?

I am ready.

The Sharman Camp is where the moon, stars and sky meet me there.

As I drive through the Mallee bush here in Australia for my annual Camping Gathering with my family, I have a deep sense to capture the essence of this moment as I enter this sacred sanctuary. As I pass over the cattle grid and gate, I am now on the red dirt track lined by ancient river red gums that immediately brings peace and calm. It takes my breath away every time being here. Almost euphoric. I drive further, and as I reach the Murray River down the dirt track, I feel cleansed – even though I have not yet been in the water physically. I feel the breeze on my face like those Ancestors' kisses on my cheek.

Soon we will light the campfire that will burn and sustain our warmth, cook our food, be the beacon of light and home while we are here. When that first flame is lit, I smell the sacred, that Earth sacred smell. That ancient smell. It hits all my senses in a single breath, and I instantly feel a strong remembering that I have returned home to Self, to Oneness and on a journey to a sacred healing Soul Spirit Space.

When I sit down by that campfire at night, the trees part in the wind and I see the stars so clearly. They shine brightly. The moon illuminates so powerfully when it is the fullest and, in those moments, I have a feeling of belonging, a Oneness. Part of the natural world, the earth below and the stars above. Not a separation. I feel my Ancestors. They remind me we are One. Not separate from. We are the water, we are the earth, we are the fire, we are the wind, we are the trees, stars and moon.

This is when I feel it most powerfully. On these annual ritual Sharman family camping trips. With my grandsons sitting beside me, having this experience and being Oneness.

I will always craft and create my new Spirit Cloth during these autumn days beside the Murray, immersed so deeply with the elements. This has become a tradition, and I will do it again next year and every other following.

Weeks later, as I drive back up the track and over the cattle grid and onto the bitumen heading towards the township, I feel cleansed, renewed, a deep gratitude and full again.

I believe there are many people who have or yearn for a deep sense of connection that can heal us in ways we didn't know we needed. Accessing the elements, being in the elements, feeling them, hearing them, seeing them is a real kind of Medicine. Being in nature, being in stillness and to just *Be*. Breathing in a deeper connection to your Inner Spirit, being and Heart. Often, to do nothing is very difficult for people, as I have witnessed in my workshops. My guests ask sometimes, 'What are we doing today or later?' I say, 'Nothing'.

This can obviously freak people out and throw them out of whack. Although when we are sitting around the campfire together or on the riverbank watching the movement, or gazing at the stars above, and having a great big belly laugh together or being in complete silence, it suddenly calms that urgent need to be doing 'things' all the time. To be in stillness and being YUMA is healing. It is really that simple.

The YUMA healing way is to live Self, Spirit and Mother *Earth*.

It really is simple.

My wish for you, the reader, is to experience this too.

Take notice.

Be aware of your surroundings.

Feel it.

Hear it.

See it.

Smell it.

Be it.

This can be the place to go physically when we need some deep connection, grounding and ceremony. We can go there also when we close our eyes.

POT OF SOUP

Ceremony starts from deep within. Sometimes a deep place that is hidden or protected and, for me, through generations. When I stand on the same place my grandparents, parents and siblings lived on the Murray riverbank surrounded by the gum trees, the place I had my first Ceremonial Sacred Smoking, *I remember, I feel, I hear and I see.*

My oldest sister Barbara told me the story that every Sunday, when she was a young child and living on the banks of the Murray River, our mother and grandmother boiled up the Medicine plants to bathe all the kids in. It was a ritual almost ceremonial.

As I drive her through the bush a year or so before she made her voyage into residential care, she is immediately emotional, smelling the bush, telling and feeling the story and memories. We always stopped and picked some leaves to rub in our hands to release the oils and bring over face, hair and arms. She remembered as we sat in silence and stillness with the windows wound down so we could smell the gums float through the car. We sat, connected and feeling it together, just watching the ripples on the water go by and the branches of the gum leaves swaying in the breeze.

She told me again about the Sandpit as we drove by and stopped briefly. It the place I have explained earlier. It is now fenced and protected. When I gather the gum leaves and river water and prepare the fire along the riverbank on this sacred place, Mother Earth, I feel healed. The intention is for healing and connection to Ancestral Songlines.

> *To be one with Mother, to*
> *celebrate, heal and honour my*
> *Songlines. There is no separation.*

Just as the generations before her, the ancient ones, our Ancestors brewed sacred pots of Medicine to feed, heal and sustain their people and tribe. My people, the Aboriginal people of Australia, nurtured the lands and waterways and ensured sustainability over thousands of years, moved in balance, and in sync and respected a deep connection with the Mother. They only took what they needed and maintained food sources throughout seasons and for future generations. The message here is to *only take what you need* and remember, 'We are all Future Ancestors, and as a Future Ancestor, we each have a responsibility to nurture, protect and restore the balance to our Mother (Earth). We are of her. She owns us. This book honours her and honours us. They were living Oneness and this *natural state and way of being*. They practised being their own Healers and the Medicine. In my dreams, I am transported back to this time to witness, feel and breathe it all in and remember the healing ways. It is truly beautiful.

I ate from the same pot of soup that was on the table each night, and that sustained my large tribe family throughout my childhood. They are the happiest memories I have as a child. My oldest sister inherited our mother's pot when she passed. My sister continued to bless that pot and create the soup that I am so connected to and feels part of my being, my Soul and Spirit. This, too, is what my brother Charlie experienced with his final bowl of chicken curry. She made many, many more pots of soup to nourish and sustain our large family tribe for generations after. That pot of soup was the best taste and happiest feeling I will ever experience. It represented belonging, hope, connection, healing, love and all together, which after much growth and healing, I would now call 'Oneness'. The soup was the Medicine. I cannot recreate that exact pot of soup of my childhood that brought all my senses alive. Making my famous pumpkin soup is my favourite thing to do to share with my guests at my workshops. However, in this modern age and world today, I am guided to create my other unique pot of soup by crafting and brewing my speciality, 'YUMA Healing Spirit Cloths', that sustains, honours and heals my being and Dreaming journey. Each brew continues to bring me back home to those early childhood pots of soup that made me feel whole.

There is something very sacred in this alchemy practice when the connection is made with Mother and all the elements. I brew the Spirit Cloths in those special sacred bush spaces my sister talks so often about along the Murray River. When I create, I have a deep knowing that takes my breath away. I remember. I am waking up. My ingredients are a fusion of healing plants and the elements. You will learn more about this further along. The pot of soup has stuck with me and continues to be a guiding metaphor in my YUMA healing practice and work today.

The pot is simply a *vessel*. Just as our body. The soup is a combination, an infusion of ingredients for consumption for nutrition, as Medicine or, for me, it is the Spirit Cloths that are my YUMA Healing Way Practice. What we put into our *pot* for consumption needs to be safe, healthy and healing and for the higher good. When there is a balance and healing intention, it is a magical alchemy infusion of transformation and creation.

Sometimes, and more and more often now, I imagine I am also a pot of soup, and what goes into my vessel, the body, needs to be safe for my physical, mind, heart and Soul Spirit healing. A remembering that I must also maintain the balance, just as generations before me were selective of what was put into the pot – mostly medicinal food and plant ingredients for nutrition or for healing Medicine. It was for all and shared with love and honour and nurtured Mother and generations. To live and be in Oneness.

JUST ADD WATER

I am a Bush and River woman from the Mallee where the Murray River flows, and red dirt runs through me, nourishes me, grounds me and heals me. Being by and a part of the Murray River is my home – my centre – it's where I draw my breath and energy.

As I sit here at my favourite spot with my coffee in the morning sun along the Murray River, I breathe in and I breathe out with a sense of uncertainty or confusion as I move through some deep release and healing. Being in this stillness and watching the ripples in the water is my meditative way. This day my senses became disturbed as the speedboats began racing by, up and down, with their motors echoing and viciously disturbing the peaceful river. Adult ducks panicking and ushering their baby family to safety. People everywhere in this usually sleepy, quiet rural town.

Visitors from the city taking up space here with their oversized boats with thunderous noisy motors, and big groups and families.

So many dogs pass me, on their leashes and behaving so well. All walking and breathing this fresh air, grinding the pavement that winds and wraps around the water's edge with their human families. Seems they have all fled the city after the regional borders opened. All seemingly searching for air, freshness, nature, purity away from the big city smoke and lockdowns. I can see a sense of freedom in their eyes as they look at me as they pas by. It seems the boaties and skiers are not aware of the dangers of the undercurrents of this ever-fast-rising Murray River, which is moving rapidly. I don't want to watch out of fear of an accident as they hoon past at a pace of 100km an hour.

The visitors not knowing the sacredness of this land and water, it saddens me.

I have a sense of grief in these moments. I remain sitting in my favourite ritual spot, not wanting to move or be forced to move with all this unwanted activity, noise and disturbance. I stay a bit longer this day to oversee the new duck family that have come out of hiding from the earlier panic and fear. I watch them walk swiftly past and down the riverbank to their safe, sacred space close by. These precious native ducks have enjoyed two years of peaceful breeding seasons during the state lockdowns. There has been no ski racing up the Murray in this time. They now seem traumatized and unsafe. This is their natural environment and their home.

Energy flowing.

Light moving through the water.

*Waves are harmonizing
the energy flow.*

*That sings to my heart
and Soul Spirit.*

On the same day, two fishermen glide peacefully past in their tinnies at a very slow walking pace. I notice them, and I know they are fishing for food. They go gently in the waterway as if not to disturb it, and it seems familiar and reminds me of an honouring of the water. The Murray River. Just as my Ancestors and family have practised to honour this source, the Murray River, which weaves and ties our Songlines, connection belonging to all tribal groups along the length of this magnificent waterway.

Macca, my brother, is a great fisherman and true bushman. He now lives in the bush at his sacred campsite and freely and happily also glides up and down the same river when fishing for his food. As a young girl, I always remember driving with my sister or aunty to the bush with my brother Macca in the car, all packed up with his swag and supplies. Then, ritually, he got out and disappeared into the past and the trees and over the creek where he stayed for months at a time. I didn't understand it at a young age and was always scared for him, but now I know he is living his true Oneness. The Murray River, the water source, is his home, heart, Spirit and Soul.

It's Just Water

When I can facilitate an Elements Spirit Cloth Creation Workshop, the day generally begins with rain. It just does. The guests will often panic and think that the day is ruined. I gently remind them, 'It is only water. It is an element, and we are here to honour all the elements in a healing way.' I will then gather my guests and start with a magical Water Ceremony.

Everyone will have their feet immersed direct in the Murray River, depending on the location of the workshop, or in sacred circle in vessels filled with gum leaves, salts, oils and Murray River water. Often tears flow once their feet are in the water. It's beautiful, cleansing and healing.

We go on a journey through the bush, the gum trees and up the river together. We imagine the Ancestors walking with us.

We smell the air and the scent of the gums.

The sacred sensations running through our bodies, our beings.

We all sit along the riverbank and watch the ripples on the water. The sun glistening and dancing like diamonds. The view takes your breath away.

The water dances around your feet and tickles the toes. Massaging and vibrating. The energy is electric and soothing at the same time.

As you all sit together and in silence, you can see and imagine the Ancestors doing the same before your time. This water source, life force, the sacred spot to gather, for ceremony and ritual, for food, for play, for creation. This water has memory, and you remember it now. You feel it flowing through you, and again your breath rises quickly, and your heart is warm, and you feel love. By now, the tears are flowing, and the remembering soothes and calms you. Deep breath in and out, in and out, in and out. It feels cleansing as if purifying your Spirit. You wriggle your toes again and feel at one with the water. You do not want to move or leave, but in that moment you hear the call of Old Man Eagle and then see him fly overhead and around you high in the sky. Your feet now leave the water, and you make your way back up to riverbank and watch in awe the sun setting and the rays of light on your face, and then they fade through the water and float up the river.

The sacred water is the first element in Creation of my YUMA Healing Spirit Cloths, and so it is placed in the water, and I then *dream it into being.* An infusion of our Ancestors' stories and love and healing. And sacred intentions to heal humanity and our Mother.

We must not fear water... it is sacred and flows through Mother to give life and bring life into being, cleansing and purifying many, many things, including our bodies inside and out.

We should and must protect, honour and always only take what we need of this vital life source. Be gentle; as a Future Ancestor, your memories will flow through and up the stream or currents just as this mystical moment.

Water is life force.

There is a sacredness, spiritual and living relationship with water through Dreaming and Songlines, a deep knowing or interconnectedness for Aboriginal people.

My people. My Ancestors.

We recognize the sacredness of our waters. We feel the connectedness of all life and their relationship to our beings.

LIGHT THE FLAME

'Wanapi' means *FIRE* in Mutti Mutti language. The essence of smoke is mystical, wise and moving. It is a connection between all realms and crosses all boundaries.

Around the campfire or in a Smoking Ceremony, we need the sacred flame, the fire.

Just as when that first flame is lit at the Sharman Annual Camp, always, always, I am transported to the sacred through smell. That earth sacred smoky smell. Ancient. A deep connection is made in an instant, and a strong remembering of a returning home to Self, Spirit and Mother Earth. Being YUMA. To my Oneness.

In my traditional Smoking Ceremony here in Australia, the gum leaves and/ or native plants of the area are placed on the flames to create that sacred smoke for cleansing, purifying and protection.

Close your eyes and connect with your breath. Take a few deep breaths as we centre ourselves here now.

I invite you to come on this YUMA journey with me now.

We are all together near the riverbank outside now and suddenly feel the WIND blowing on our faces. We hear the trees rustling and the branches crunch under our feet. We are all now in bush on this SACRED LAND. We are surrounded by the beautiful eucalyptus trees with their leaves blowing in the wind; it feels so serene surrounded by River Red Gums. We look around and notice they line the river edge for as far as we can see.

We hear a whistle, and look to the sky... it's the Eagle, he leaves his tree on the opposite side of the river and flies towards us, he sings out and welcomes us to this Space.

He remembers us and flies over and around the treetops. Then glides back to his tree, where he observes.

We continue and collect some branches of gum leaves from the ground and gently walk towards the water. There is a small ceremony FIRE burning. We place our leaves on top of the gentle flames.

We smell that sweet eucalyptus scent and the smoke dancing around us. We open our arms out front towards the smoke to catch it and bring it up over our crown, then sweep our arms down around our feet. It feels so soothing, calming and grounding. The scent stays with us.

BE ONE with this space. Hold this space for you, your being in this moment.

What is your STORY – YOUR DREAMING?

What is it?

Breathe it in, feel it all the way to your heart space.

Are you happy with your STORY JOURNEY so far?

HAVE YOU GOT A NEW STORY? DO YOU WANT TO CHANGE YOUR STORY?

What needs to be celebrated? Honoured? Forgiven? Released? Remembered?

What is the healing energy you need to hear, feel, see or know right now?

What is it?

What is the message you've been waiting to receive?

Reflect in this moment if you have been blocking or ignoring these messages.

Do you feel that you could be holding pain, uncertainty, guilt, grief, shame, sadness, anger, frustration in that deep, deep place that only you know about?

It could also be floating on the surface, ready and waiting to be dealt with.

You may also feel empty.

What DO YOU NEED? What are you waiting for?

What is your Soul telling you right now? Listen.

Do you hear a whisper?

If not a whisper, a knowing, a feeling that feels like hope.

Take notice of your breath now... Every breath here now is supporting your intention for your healing story. Dreaming moving forward.

Our gentle breaths are creating THE ENERGY AND CONNECTION to our Ancestors. My Ancestors. Your Ancestors who have GATHERED us all here to connect and be in this very moment.

We are now breathing with them right here. THE ONE BREATH, THE SAME BREATH. Breathing in Oneness, we are becoming Oneness.

Hold your heart – remember this feeling, these breaths, the whispers, the knowing.

You hear the Eagle now flying over you. It's time.

YOUR DREAMING NOW is to take this energy and infuse and breathe that sense of knowing, that sense of hope into your journey. Resonate in that energy, be creative, tell the story, sing that song, dance to that rhythm of hope and intention and of truth. Heal it, live it, breathe it and BE it.

BE YUMA. Just BE.

Enjoy your journey forward and remember you can visit here anytime to a YUMA sacred space to soothe your heart, nurture your Soul, restore balance and renew hope.

Yumila Kiyaka.

A motion of connection.

A movement of healing

A continual breath.

A Oneness.

I'm wondering where to start the writing of this part of the story today, and Spirit guides me to the song 'Dancing in the Dark' that suddenly comes on and the lyrics, 'Can't start a fire without a spark.'

So that is where I will start.

When I am camping or at one of my Spirit Cloth Creation Workshops, there is always a designated Firekeeper. Sometimes it's me, my daughter Jessica or my grandson, Johnathon. When that first spark creates that flame and the fire builds, the energy is electric and transformative and hopeful. You can feel it in the air. There will be some great, profound, healing shifts and releases today. It's just a feeling.

YUMA Spirit Cloth Creation

Join me on the riverbank beside the ancient gum trees when the moon is full. For we will create a new way. Connect and Be Self,

Spirit and Mother Earth. We will become our own Healers and Medicine. We will become YUMA and Oneness.

Fire represents willpower, inner strength and transformation through action, transformational and purifying powers.

As the Cloths are wrapped, and healing intentions are spoken and Dreamed into them, they will be placed in my big YUMA pot with the gum leaves, plants and Murray River water. The pot has been brewing gently and heated enough for the water to roll over and dance with the Medicine of the plants. The full moon is usually shining down on the proceedings, and the energy of the group is rising. The Cloths begin to gently dance in the brewing pot that is gently infusing the Ancestors' stories and all you wished for.

I gather the circle once more to sit and observe their thoughts and reflections in silence as the Cloths are rolling around the pot, being infused with natural bush dye and Plant Medicine and healing energy, and alchemized in love and intention. The YUMA Spirit Cloth is coming into Being.

Around the circle is now the time to offer reflections and, as I explain, the YUMA way. When we apply that gentle pressure just as we have with flame and fire together with the water, it resembles a 'pot of soup'. What happens is some floaties, residue or shit rises to the top. It just sits there stirring up our emotions and thoughts.

All that sticky, toxic, shitty shit stuff. That no longer serves us in any way. That has no purpose in our future.

We can be gentle here if more time is needed to release, or we can 'turn it up' and boil the shit away.

Only when the group is ready will we move in sync to that place together, holding space, holding each other. The firekeeper adds the new log to the fire, and again the flames are ignited and are now roaring.

Roaring, boiling, brewing, purifying, releasing, cleansing and renewing. We watch in awe. We hear those whispers again, reminding and remembering we are enough. We are hope, we are love. Our Cloths are calling and singing in the new. A new way of being. And are transformed and alchemized into the **YUMA Spirit Cloth**.

AIR – WIND

The air and the wind come in waves, at the right time and in a divine way.

Just as we take our Spirit Cloths out of the YUMA brew pot, you feel the wind on your cheeks, through your hair, as if the Ancestors' kisses are circling and celebrating you in this magical moment.

You breathe in and smell the Medicine. The sweet, sacred scent is taking you closer and closer home. You find some refuge and space to sit quietly and breathe it all in. Tears flow as your breath rises and rises and flows in sync. It's a surreal sensation you haven't felt before. A newness.

You are excited to unravel your Spirit Cloth. Patterns, lines and images only you can see are waiting for you. Just as unique as you are. Your heartbeat, your breath, healing and your Dreaming.

As you have created and unravelled your YUMA Spirit Cloth, your Being will rest, breathe, connect, heal, and restore balance to integrate a nurturing vibrational practice of lasting self-care.

THE RISE

We will rise together and move together. We will walk home together. Stronger, connected, hopeful, proud, grounded and in the light. Away from darkness, fear, shame, hate, sadness, grief. All those shitty things that kept holding you back. You have a way forward. You just had to stand still long enough to be found. You are here now, nurtured, and you are free.

YUMA Healing Way through Ceremony and the Spirit Cloth

Earth is the element of calm, control and thoughtful contemplation.

Water represents emotion, intuition, fluidity and intelligence.

Air is intellect, intention and a connection to life force.

Fire represents willpower, inner strength and transformation through action.

When all the elements combine, it is a perfect balance of all there is, and with this balance, it is the Oneness; it is harmony.

And, in this, not forgetting the human element – our human Spirit. The thread that alchemizes all the elements to share in nature's beauty.

YUMA

WISDOM WHISPERS

Be Spirit

Spirit guides me, moves and dances through me and leads me.

Growing up, I was often afraid of what Spirit was. I always heard scary 'things', and I still hear them today from my people and others. It is sometimes the unspoken thing to talk about. I feel now, at my age, that Spirit is very sacred. My Soul Spirit is one and the same. More specific is a 'force' that is and belongs to your Being, an energy, or consciousness. Creation. A Oneness.

Telling and writing my story has allowed me to recognize how my Soul Spirit played a vital role in my life. My protection and survival as a little Black orphan girl. The scary things that we were warned about, I guess, were a sense of protection and not to mess with 'Spirit', or other versions of Spirit that had no place in my existence.

The Thread of Spirit

The thread of Spirit weaves through us.

She spins through nature, tying together the elements linking us with Ancestors.

And in our returning, we can follow the Spirit thread home.

She is the invisible strands that catch the light at dawn. She is always there. She always was.

PART THREE

Immersion

Here I am, I am Here, I found Me.

This section is made up of the following chapters. In it, you, the reader, will be guided to unearth your way home to yourself and live in honour of the Earth and the Ancestors.

- Let Us Weave

- Let Your Spirit Show You

- New Threads and Hooks: Catching On

- Listen

'Here I am, I have arrived.

I am here, I heard you.

I honour you, I honour me.'

ANNABELLE SHARMAN

In this section, the Spirit Weaver shares guidance of YUMA, the thread of Spirit and the threads of connection.

Those 'aha' moments can take us by surprise and, at times, take our breath away. When we can be still and just BE, we let Spirit show us the way. We may notice more and more of these moments; we then become more in tune, attuned and aligned.

LET US WEAVE

Mungo Footsteps

May you Connect and be grounded to Mother Earth while you walk on this Sacred Land.

BE still, present and connect.

Recently I drove to Mungo, which is by far one of the most spiritual and cultural places. It is so powerful, nurturing. When I arrive on the outskirts of the dry lakes that form the Mungo National Park, I feel and sense I am being transported to another realm. Another time and another age. Miles from anywhere and desert-like. Many hundreds of miles up the track from the Murray River and my hometown. However, this place is traditional country for me as a Mutti Mutti woman. It is so obviously ancient, the look, the feel, the dust, the dirt and the air. The dunes are like ancient pinnacles, and the colours of sun setting or rising is ethereal. When the full moon rises over the dunes is a magical sight to witness. But just being here in the daylight or feeling the full moon bathing you in an energetic shower that flows through your body is magical, spiritual and scary. And you have a deep sense that Ancients are here watching your every move. You would not dare take a step in the wrong direction. Wildlife – the kangaroos and emus – are at home here, this mystical cultural playground. I can sit and watch and watch and breathe this vision in all day and night and be mesmerized in another time.

I remember as a young adult, not long after becoming a new mother, travelling there with Elders for a day trip. I heard the whispers then, and it scared me. I did not dare walk past the gate on the ancient dunes; it is too sacred and, as an Aboriginal person, seems so disrespectful.

I had many planned trips to Mungo with friends that didn't take place because of bad weather and lockdowns. And I felt a deeper, more meaningful reason – it was because Mungo Man and Mungo Lady had not returned home there to be reburied.

> *'Mungo Lady and Mungo Man, found resting just*
> *metres apart, were buried more than 42,000 years*
> *ago on Lake Mungo's shores. The planet's oldest*

> *ritual burials, Mungo Lady was cremated, Mungo*
> *Man adorned with ochre. They represent the early*
> *emergence of human spiritual beliefs and provide*
> *a glimpse into the care provided to kin through*
> *Australia's deep history. Along with 20,000-year-old*
> *fossil human footprints, they tell an incredible*
> *story of First Australians' long history and led to*
> *the establishment of Mungo National Park.'*

It was as though Spirit had guided me with this, and I had to trust it. So, I was travelling back not too long ago, as a grandmother this time. I had been moving through some deep, deep healing. I walked gently and wisely on this sacred earth once I arrived.

I wrapped my Spirit Cloth around me, and my daughter Jessica wiped me with ochre as if I was ready for ceremony. I was there. I was home, and my tears rolled as I felt the Ancient ones move and breathe through me. It took my breath away over and over. The tears connected me with the beginning of time. Just as my Elders told me, this place. Mungo. I stood there in silence and closed my eyes. The Eagles flew overhead, the wind circled me and whispered through me. I breathed the gentle breath in harmony as a Mutti Mutti Aboriginal woman, coming home, being home and being life and being as One with Mother.

The thread of Spirit
weaves through us.

She spins through nature,
tying together the elements
linking us with Ancestors.

And in our returning, we follow
the Spirit thread home.

She is the invisible strands
that catch the light at dawn.

She is always there. She always was.

*I breathe with my Ancestors when I close
my eyes and dream. They guide me to
create the Rhythm of Light to heal Mother
Earth, my people and humanity.*

I stand here as a Future Ancestor. My footsteps are peace, and my breath is knowledge, and my words are wisdom. And just like that, in a breath, I moved off the ancient dunes to protect her and continue to walk with honour and respect for her here and everywhere my feet touch the ground. I feel stronger, balanced and centred walking away from this land. It was just what my Spirit needed. It was like the Ancestors blessed me, initiated me and showed me the way home to Self.

My heart is full of love; I feel so in love with life.

*Breathing the same breath as my Ancestors is
my centre, my heart, my Soul, my home.*

LET YOUR SPIRIT SHOW YOU

The thread of connection links us to the now, to our future and to our Ancients. It is the Soul, the Breath, the Spirit.

As we unravel and introduce our YUMA Spirit Cloths to the sky, the sun and full moon above, we imagine that the Ancestors are receiving with love all the intentions made during its creation. As the Cloth floats through the air over and over again, the sun's rays gently find your face and the warm glow is embracing you and sends tingles through your body all the way to your toes. These are the sacred moments I witness in Self and others as they unravel and bring their Spirit Cloth home. It's magical, emotional, spiritual, and healing in so many ways.

Tears often rise and flow. And knees often kiss the ground when overcome with emotion and this new feeling that is unexplainable. The 'aha's over and over again. The connections. The honouring, the remembering, the love that feels like home. It feels brand new and yet so familiar.

You see Spirit in your Cloth; you see you in your Cloth. You see your intentions in your Cloth.

It all makes sense now. It's what you Dreamed into it. You sacredly embrace your Spirit Cloth bringing it to your face, and then rest it on your heart space and breathe it all in. Breathe in, breathe out, breathe in, breathe out. It all makes sense now. You feel, see, breathe it all in over and over all while your knees are hugging Mother Earth like a magnet and connecting those vibrations from you and your Spirit Cloth.

You stay here for a while and suddenly look around.

As you take a look around, you realize that you may not be alone. You sense that the Ancestors are here too. You feel them here with you so strongly now. You smell the smoke from the fire as if calling your name. Your senses know to step forward and intuitively place your leaves and foliage onto the flames. You ceremonially bless the fire with your leaves. You feel the vibration in the leaves move through you; they hold your Dreaming. The steamy smoke and smell hit your awareness suddenly, and you stand there holding your Cloth up to receive its blessing and smoking. You stand in harmony and in sacred circle with your Ancestors, all together; it feels like you become part of the smoke. A sense of no separation, an immersion into Oneness. In Oneness and in Continual breath. Your Ancestors are dancing with you, renewing, cleansing, celebrating, and creating this new alignment.

You embody this moment. The confirmations and that deep remembering are singing to your heart, Spirit and deeply to your Soul. The vibrations under your feet are anchoring and connecting to Mother beneath where you stand. Becoming stronger. An empowered strength moves deeply through your body.

Breathing in and out with a calmness you have not felt before. A lightness. Inviting and returning your balance to your centre and in alignment with Source, with Self, Spirit and Mother Earth. In this space, you feel so held and protected, safe in the sacred and with every breath while the smoke is circling and blessing your Being, you are embracing and becoming inner peace, love and Oneness.

This Smoking Ceremony cleanses, removes negative energy and, in many tribes, welcomes you to the land.

The essence of ceremonial smoke is sacred, mystical, wise and meets you where you are here and now.

It is a connection between all realms and crosses all boundaries.

Creating, aligning, and remembering pathways for your Dreaming and your future.

Dancing Eagles and Crystals

As I take a new adventure with my dear friend Lea to the mountain retreat, I am suddenly transported into a new environment I am not used to, coming from the Mallee dry bush. The air is different, the animals, the trees, the soil and the water. The water I see in the distance is seawater, the ocean. We are perched high in this private sanctuary retreat. It's so peaceful. The house is high on the mountain and accessed by winding gravel roads around the mountain. I felt like I was travelling to a new spiritual height. Deep down, I knew something significant and special would happen as I was searching for that *word* to explain the meaning I was experiencing. We enjoyed vodka shots (a very rare occasion), fresh-caught sea fish and candlelight as the raging storms had taken out the power. I was a little uneasy as this is not my country, and I could feel the Ancestors' presence surrounding the mountain. I remembered very clearly that I had to present myself and acknowledge the ancient ones, the land, the animals, the elements of the place where I stood. It's what I must do and is my practice as an Aboriginal person when

I travel to and through other tribal boundaries. In that moment, I had a sense of being welcomed and felt calmer and more at peace.

As this was a new area for me, I was a tourist, and we moved through the landscape during the day. We visited a crystal warehouse on the way. I feel as though I always find these special places where there is always a piece that stops you in your tracks. I was overwhelmed by the energy and the collection; it was amazing. I rummaged through the rough pieces as I always do and are generally my preference – a bit rough around the edges, just like me. I did a lap and another, and just as I was about to make a purchase and out of nowhere, I mean it was as if Spirit placed this rough crystal on the counter in front of me from the scrap basket. It was a large piece of Tiger's Eye, it was rough, and I admired the shape. It was like a teardrop. Oh, so I purchased it for $5. Tiger's Eye is my power crystal, as I learned years earlier while completing my Crystal Therapy course and training. I did not have a personal piece yet, but I dreamed of having a piece as a necklace that touched my skin.

As we continued to drive down the mountain, I felt this word arise within me. That word was *Oneness*. It was not a word I used. However, as I heard it deeper and louder within my being, I realized that this word was who I was becoming or returning to. The following morning and after the huge storm, I was introduced to one of the caretakers on the property who was restarting the power. A gifted man of many trades, I learned. Well, one of his trades is silversmith and jewellery making. He asked me if I would like to have the crystal polished. He will return it to me before I go. We continued our adventures and, on this day, drove further away from the mountain to a nearby village. When we came to a sudden stop. In the air to our left beside the road were two magnificent Wedge-tail Eagles dancing the sacred dance together. They flew towards us and over, and then we saw more. We were speechless. It seemed this was performed specifically for us in that moment. I could see the Eagle's eyes as he flew closer. It happened in a moment, and both me and friend Lea were mesmerized and felt joy to experience this rare moment. I knew this was a sign to confirm that word that had risen up earlier as I made my way around and down the mountain.

I met some wonderful and spiritual wise people on this exciting day looking out over the waters and ocean view. To be honest, I felt as though they were greeted by and speaking directly to my Soul and Ancestors. I felt very seen and held in this special space and continue to have a respectful friendship with the ladies I met.

The day came to leave, and again, the caretaker appeared out of nowhere, and he presented me with a necklace. Oh my God.

He had polished the Tiger's Eye, wrapped it in silver casing and woven kangaroo skin and sealed it into this unique piece. Especially for me. I was absolutely in awe and shocked, and overwhelmed, humbled that someone would want to be so kind and offer this custom, very special spiritual gift. He did not know that Tiger's Eye was my power crystal. I write wearing this necklace most of the time and when I do my workshops.

This trip was much needed and a guiding experience that was a catalyst for my own healing and for my healing work in the future. I trusted and was open to receive the sign or confirmation I was waiting for, a sign that would inspire and support me as I embarked on a process to transform and integrate my own healing growth and share the gifts and offerings of Oneness. I wore that necklace on a regular basis while creating my business.

NEW THREADS AND HOOKS:
CATCHING ON

Thread the magic and lead at point. Through the eyelet and looping back into itself.

Perforating holes along the way to enable the thread to be received.

We must be in order to receive.

To be is our meaning, our being, our doing, our knowing. To be is presence – is seeing and hearing, it is to gather and be in circle.

To be expands our capacity to weave through intention, heart and ancestral knowing.

To be illuminates the thread that together is us. Because together we are woven.

We are not lost; we are must returning.

So here we are in the now. As an Aboriginal person, I have strong connections that link me to the ancient – the beginning of time. However, when trauma happens, and for me, it was colonization, here in Australia, those links become damaged. And Aboriginal people, part of a whole collective, have to continually thread and weave our way back home. I often hear Healers say to release and heal, we must 'cut cords'. We never would sever or cut that cord or link because, if we did that, it would destroy completely the connection to our Songlines and Dreaming. We have to and must heal the links or the threads. For my people healing means regenerating and reigniting many cultural practices that have been disturbed since colonization in Australia. We are not a lost people – we are just weaving our way back home.

So, new creations of daily vibrational practice support and keep the thread strong and energized. This can be true for all people, and I share my wisdom and knowledge of Earth Medicine and healing with many. We as humanity need to be and do better, and this includes for a healing of Mother Earth.

Every new link, weave, new awareness, breath, every new footstep and hop, skip and jump on Mother Earth, is a ripple of change, hope and healing. A vibration of love to reach a deep place of your heart and to Mother Earth.

To BE

Is our meaning,

Our being,

Our doing,

Our knowing.

I often reflected on the earlier chakra workshop and Reiki training that was a strong part of my activation. Over many, many years, I can remember a clearing and cleansing process moving through my body and being. Almost like each energy centre being unblocked not just once but many times. I was drawn to the crystal shops in the towns either side of me, both along the Murray River. I also realized I only bought crystals from towns with large bodies of water, such as the Murray or oceans. It's just my thing that I trust and honour in me.

It is important here to note that I mentioned earlier clearing my energy centres or chakras many times. Yes, many times. I found to be true that this energy practice is one that means we need to maintain a balance and strive to live an embodied life that supports balance, and I can just BE YUMA. When I am that, I can live Oneness.

I was creating my Medicine bag as my love of Plant Medicine and oils began or was remembered, just as the connection with gum leaves. And the oils became a part of my Medicine Bag, and I use them daily for grounding, balancing, coming home to my centre and – since writing – for focus and release. I have many items in my bag, which travels with me always.

It was as though a continual breath of healing confirmations were occurring at a rapid but safe pace and draped in my Spirit Cloth.

I now had an open and cleared channel to the Ancestors.

I was dancing and swaying to the rhythm of the Ancestral heartbeat.

I was Dreaming new dreams and believing they were possible.

I was understanding the need for protecting energy to avoid burnout or depletion.

I was finding and becoming an inner peace that I can only remember the day I was lifted out of the makeshift cot by my aunty when I was a new baby and the day of my only birthday party when I was a little girl living on Ronald Street. In a continual breath of change, I was becoming Oneness.

My practice is based around the water and specifically the Murray River, where I was born and have lived all my life. I sit by the riverbank each morning. It brings stillness and calms me. I didn't realize how much the river meant to me. Although I grew up and was always at the river with friends swimming at the ramp or with family on fishing and swimming trips. It was when I had my Smoking Ceremony, which was at the space where my grandparents and parents' family lived in the bush on the Murray River. This event changed my life. It activated a deeper level of connection like no other. The water from that river holds memory. All the memories before time, the Ancestors from the beginning of time and cycles of Mother Earth. I suddenly felt that this all runs within me now.

The more I connected with the water and this element, the more I became healed and gained strength and confidence to create the YUMA Healing and Spirit Cloth practice.

YUMA is just like the Murray River,
a movement in healing.

I was healing myself and others in ways I did not realize possible. The naturalness and the power of the water. It is like the Ancestors' nectar blessing us when we show up for ourselves. You can hear the Ancestors' whispers in this place. It's alive. Providing this gentle essence that is freely available and accessible. Just be here. Breathe in the breeze and the feel of the dew from the river in the early mornings is the best.

I strongly feel the Spirit Weaver energy gaining insight and intuition when I am in this space, and it embodies the healing of just BE.

My Aboriginal community have a big gathering here each year during the Easter holidays, which is the beginning of autumn here in Australia. The time when the first campfires are lit and just being here is the Medicine. Elders reminisce, and all the kids are lined up along the riverbank fishing. There's lots of cooking and yarning and laughing. The whole gathering is healing in itself for so many.

> ***When I sit on the riverbanks of the Murray,***
> ***I sit on the laps of our Ancestors.***

This is the water that I create my Spirit Cloths with and which the people who come along to make their custom Cloths immerse their feet into during the water ceremony. And when the pots are brewed, this sacred water is the main ingredient to alchemize the healing Medicine Spirit Cloths.

I was always at the river. For fun, when a teenager, swimming at the ramp each day in summer, with family and ceremony. I would not say I was a great at fishing, but I always enjoyed being present there, just watching and breathing in the water. My husband and I always took our young kids to the river, and they have been camping since babies during Easter holiday in autumn. It's kind of a tradition now where they bring their kids – my grandchildren – to enjoy and embody this special sacredness. My son found himself fishing alongside his father.

I have a very special photo of me as a baby, almost one year old, with my father holding my hand on the riverbank, showing me the water. From the same day, there is another photo of both my parents, brother Charlie, sister Joanne just being a family and enjoying Being. My favourite and most prized photos. Joanne and I always laugh at a specific photo taken on the same day of both of us sitting by the trunk of this giant red gum tree. Both little ones. We always say we will recreate that photo one day soon.

Yabbying would have to be the best fun memories. Always an annual event and always memorable. Catching yabbies (freshwater crustaceans for our international readers) on a line or in a net with fresh meat as bait. Going with my Aunty Lil and Uncle Buck or my brothers Macca and Charlie and sister Emily. Although getting pinched by a yabby is not fun! But sliding and slipping around in the mud and water was the ultimate fun a bush kid can have. I didn't know then those yabbies bury themselves to conserve energy, mate and protect themselves.

We always, as a big family tribe, would go out after the floodwater receded. The feast to follow was the best and always shared with the whole family. I would prefer yabbies over lollies any day now, it seems.

Being here, immersed in and with the water on this land where I stand, live and dream, I feel the energy, the history, the Dreaming, the memories of generations and generations before me, my

Ancestors. This water is and was back then the life source – force that sustained tribes along the river and waterways. They only took what they needed and managed the health of water through the seasons.

The Murray is resilient like its people. It is resourceful,
flowing, alive, breathing, nurturing, honest and cleansing.

The river teaches us to listen, to Be. To know equalness to all.
To understand change and direction and to know boundaries.

We learn from her about detachment for
greater flows and selfless service.

As the river widens and deepens over time so must we.

She encourages us to rest on her inner spring of love and share her reassurance of Ancestors' breath that are the ripples across the surface of her waters.

Come.

Be.

Hear the gentle lapping upon the riverbank. Experience the waves of possibility that are here for you always.

LISTEN

To BE illuminates the thread that together is us. Because together we are woven.

When the YUMA Spirit Cloth is unravelled and blessed in ceremony, and it finds you and drapes your physical body, we wait and listen for our love messages and intentions to be said back to us. But we have to listen deeply.

What do you mean by this?

Aboriginal people and culture has a practice of deep listening; it is almost a spiritual skill based on respect for our environment. Some call it 'Dadirri', meaning deep listening is inner, quiet. Still awareness, waiting.

When we can sit in stillness and hear with intention, we may hear those Divine messages.

Listen to the whispers that are calling your name.

Calling you home and returning you home.

Sign after sign. Confirming, calling you, encouraging you, empowering you and waking you up.

Spirit weaving and travelling through you. You must listen.

A thought.

A feeling.

A moment.

Being in your centre.

Moving to the rhythm, dancing to the music only you can hear.

Those 'aha' moments can take us by surprise and, at times, take our breath away. When we can be still and just BE, we let Spirit show us the way. We may notice more and more of these moments, we tap into our strength, and we then become more in tune, attuned and aligned.

Being a space holder for our own Self is one of the biggest challenges we have as humans. It requires us to use all our senses and to listen is a priority. It does not necessarily mean listening with our ears. It also means, in a spiritual and energetic sense, listening through our bodies, actions, other people's actions, and through Mother Earth and the elements. The space we hold for Self and others is a continual breath filled with confirmations that allow us to create new threads, to weave healing, to dance, to dream, to be brave, to create, to channel, to protect and to move towards inner peace and love. As a Social Worker, Practitioner and Counsellor, I must hold space for others and the way I do that is listening to what is not being said. Often that is where the trauma is hiding and finding a way through for healing.

To BE is presence, is seeing and hearing;
it is to gather and be in circle.

When we listen, it is as though Spirit, Ancestors and higher source are leaving a trail of breadcrumbs for us to follow to a deeper connection with our own Spirit, Soul and healing.

Listen to:

- Body

- Environment

- Elements

- Animals

We are attuned or in tune.

YUMA

WISDOM WHISPERS

Be Mother Earth

Be where you are, feel Mother, her essence, her breath, her vibe.

Move with her, BE in sync with her.

Protect her.

We are all her.

We came from the soil and will return to the soil, we are the same, and we are One.

As I stand in stillness in the lake with no one in sight or witness, I feel the water and the mud on my feet and in my toes. Grounded and still.

My immersed body craved the cold cleansing water to wash over me.

The water moves around me, and I move in sync with the flow.

Swaying, breathing, being at one with the water.

The clear blue sky above as far as the eye can see.

The old man Eagle greets me now and
circles me for a little while.

I feel a renewal balance coming through me.
I feel the breath of my Ancestors.

Breathing the same breath as my Ancestors is
my centre, my heart, my Soul, my home.

I feel the Oneness embodying me.

I am Oneness.

It doesn't matter if you are in the middle of the bush, around the campfire, in your office, bedroom, in a temple, in a sacred place in a faraway land, in another country from your birth. Welcome yourself here now. Land your feet, your breath, your body and greet Mother Earth where you are. Feel at one with her. Bless her and yourself at the same time. This is where you want to be at home and belong. Be respectful and pay reverence to her and, most importantly, to the First peoples – the traditional owners of the area. Know who they are.

We have to and must welcome ourselves here now, or we will continue to feel we do not belong. Moving through a lifetime of shame and guilt, or as I have seen and witnessed in my gatherings, colonized white shame and guilt. Choose now to be that change and respect that is much needed on Mother Earth.

One of my most profound healing moments with my guests and clients has been when I move people out of their mind and body space of not belonging to the land and bring them home. Welcoming them and allowing them to welcome themselves and arrive at a sense of belonging and safety. Being a part of Mother Earth is a need we all must feel and embody. To have an immersion experience is a gift and when it happens, often brings tears of love and freedom, respect and acceptance. An honouring of the First peoples and traditional custodians is an everlasting healing result.

- What is needed for you to feel welcome to the land where you are?

- How will being welcomed make you feel?

- How will you honour the First peoples and traditional owners – custodians?

- What difference can you make?

We can all be custodians of Mother Earth. Don't be confused, though. Traditional owners and First peoples have a unique role and must be respected, recognized and acknowledged.

This is the balance that is much needed and one that humanity must play a role in restoring. One that doesn't include blowing and blasting sacred sites and tearing through Mother Earth as if we have another to go to.

We are interconnected with all that lives and breathes and with all that does not.

PART FOUR

Peace

This section is made up of the following chapters:

- Safe Sacred Space

- What Do You Mean Be Grounded?

- How Will I Know?

In it, you, the reader, will be guided about what safe, sacred space may look like for individuals and how we are in the world through our work. I will share my experiences of how I developed a deeper relationship with the Earth so that you can always feel grounded. What safe, sacred space can be and how we can feel safe and protected in positive ways and share ways of stepping out of the darkness and into love. Finding a positive safe Soul Spirit space to be grounded and walk Mother Earth. Along the journey, you/we may experience being stronger, wiser, healthier, loved, alive and a Soul Spirit-connected life.

> *'There is no separation. There is no division.*
> *We have a feeling, and that is our knowing.'*

SAFE SACRED SPACE

Living in the darkness throughout my life since a young girl became my sacred space; it was safety for me. Reflecting now as an adult, the darkness was that horrible place that breeds despair, hate, fear and all things not love. I have experienced this most of my life, and still, to this day, that darkness can haunt me. I can now admit after 50 years Earthside, I once used the darkness as protection and became best friends with it. I bathed in the glory of pain, suffering, guilt and shame. All the while hiding from myself – dying of numbness, allowing my history to destroy me by suffocating me and bouncing and rolling me through this lifetime, bump after hard bump. I didn't know any different. I didn't know love. I wasn't living a *YUMA* way of life. My life became all about safety, surviving and then, later in life, I learned to Surrender.

How I Found My Safe Sacred Space

It feels as though the biggest battle of all time is with Self. We need to break through the invisible cage we place ourselves in for protection. For me, it was just like that damn Tweety-bird. The cage can silence and numb our voice and poison our footsteps to a healthy life and continue to tether us to that unhealthy negative space. Life can then become all about avoiding, escaping, and struggling to survive emotionally, physically, and spiritually. Your purpose becomes trapped in this pattern of destruction and harm.

When I became brave enough to take control of my trauma story, to release to Spirit and call in my Ancestors and to surrender to all the messy, murky, dark, shitty shit stuff that had to be released, I completely deeply surrendered. I completely surrendered to trust, and felt safe to be cleansed through my Aboriginal traditional Smoking Ceremony healing way, and I was stripped bare of all the pain, grief and trauma that I have carried for 40-plus years.

I was able to stand in the stillness and heal. I mean real healing that reached very deep dark places of my Soul Spirit and the physical world. I felt cleansed as if I had been blasted with a pressure washer from the inside out.

'...sometimes we forget where home and our sacred space is... it's within us...'

ANNABELLE SHARMAN

This part of my human story feels so surreal. I am living out these final chapters of this very book in real life, it seems. The new meaning and naming of this section 'Peace' is a path to finding freedom and healing into Oneness. As mentioned earlier in the story, safety has always been a priority for me. At times in my lifetime, I have protected and blocked my own energy. Thinking that's how I should live and be safe. In fact, what I was doing to my being was shutting myself down and regurgitating fear and sabotaging happiness over and over again. When you live with trauma and intergenerational trauma all your life, for me, it became a habit. This is the normal. This was my safety.

Over the past number of years, I have been experiencing great change in the way I exist in the world, in my body, in my healing work, relationships and how I connect with others.

During this time, I had this strong vibrational pull to search for, seek and learn about sacred space. I questioned... What is sacred space? Where is it? And how do we know we have it!?

Spirit was throwing me a life jacket and lifeline and weaving me back home. I experienced some clear and focused guidance and many 'aha' moments about sacred space. My experiences were becoming clearer and more authentic as my definition and sense of *safe* were no longer contaminated.

My newly created business and healing practice was transforming into new directions, and changes were occurring at a rapid pace. I began to trust this deep knowing. I was reminded that my Dreaming is on the path – to trust your inner knowing – and importantly, my sacred space is wherever I am. It is inside me; I AM MY SACRED SPACE! It's my heart, my breath, my Soul. My choice and healing that I have gifted to Self. It was not the four walls of my then healing room or office, it's ME.

It was very clear how I move in the world and how I Be in the world from now was my new Medicine. As my healing practice and work were being transformed and developing, there was a strong deep realization that I had to be my own Healer and the Medicine. It all made sense now. As written earlier about my work practices, this is exactly what I was empowering, inspiring and encouraging in clients. The more I was healing and becoming my safe, sacred space, the deeper healing work I was doing and could share and empower with others. And importantly, I also started to see myself as others saw me.

I believed that the way I worked with clients in my therapeutic work and the energy and respect I shared was what I needed most for myself. I just did not know it at the time.

And I was the only one to do that, or I sought out (or my Spirit did) the people who are part of holding healing energy and safety for me on my journey.

So as a way of surrendering, releasing and clearing and removing those cages or high walls allows and calls in others to walk with you on your healing path. Almost like a new healing shield is being built surrounding you that is fluid, free, safe and sacred but where you gain strength and stability. And you get to define your new safe, your new sacred. It's a beautiful place to be energetically, physically, emotionally and spiritually. One that I have experienced on my own journey.

The people who are called into your journey form a shield of healing surrounding you. They see in you and shine a light on what you cannot see in yourself. They fan the flames that ignite the fire for you to rise and become who you are meant to be. Like dying and coming back to life. A newness that you may not have experienced before. I am personally scared of balloons and the fear of letting them go. We hold on for dear life to those things, right?! Particularly helium balloons, because we don't know where they will end up or where the wind will take them. It is the unknown. This is what deep healing is! We do not know what is on the other side or where we will end up either.

Being in my body and living in my body from within. YUMA is about being home – we are home, and we must live from within and not be tricked, believe we must and have to live in a material world. Life starts with our breath, our heart and love. That is a place where we should be encouraged to live from.

Surrendering and letting go of fear, being braver and trusting will be one of the biggest events or experiences. I began experiencing this newness in many ways, such as the following on my personal journey.

- Creating safe.

- Creating new sacred space.

- Creating and shifting and flowing into a healthful change, habits, practices and behaviours.

- Creating connections to Self.

- Being in environments that vibrate and resonate with you and support and hold you.

- Feeling in your physical body or feeling your body for the first time.

- Emotionally experiencing a new kind of peace and safety.

- Spiritually opening or being guided to new teachings and learnings.

- Connections around relationships are being dissolved, and new connections being made.

- Peace and freedom being felt.

- Sacred space is safety.

- Security and preservation.

- A reminder of YUMA and sense of safety of being home and being safe.

- Balanced.

- Self-care Ceremony.

- Why has PEACE been so important to me?

- How can WE embody Peace?

How I Maintain and Protect My Safe, Sacred Space Energy

A part of protecting our energy is rest and stillness. At least that was what I had practised. Recently after two years of living through a pandemic and being in lockdowns, I planned and went on retreat to the ocean interstate when I was finally allowed to travel and move freely.

I did nothing. NO work, writing, meetings, zooms. Much reading was had, and visioning for the future. Meals were prepared from the garden crops, and coffee made to order each day. Having great conversations with loved ones and reaching new levels of understanding my own silence and what that means for deeper meanings for me spiritually, emotionally, culturally, and physically in my body. I stayed in this state for one month.

What I noticed after a week and a bit was that my being was feeling free. There was not any anxiety running through my system. I could finally name it – anxiety. I felt lighter each day. As if each knot had been unravelled day by day. My energy became what I cannot really describe because it was a *new* that I had not experienced before.

I felt the darkness dissolve from my being. It is time. It was time, and it was long overdue. I had to find a new friend and divorce myself from that dark stuckness, despair and fear.

This moment I woke up and felt different, felt light, and felt free. It was a pure gift and I cried pure healing tears. I talked to my Mother Spirit in silence, and I cried with her also. I cried and thanked my higher Self. It was a new feeling, one I had not witnessed and experienced in my life ever.

Just as the unravelling of the Spirit Cloth. The knots and threads had all been untwined, cut loose or regenerated and made into new threads of connection, love, safety, stability and strength.

I arrived back home on the Murray River feeling a new energy within me.

One day I drove to the lake and sat and observed the wind blowing through the peppercorn trees and giant ancient gums. The waves lapping the sand on the lake's edge.

It seemed so majestic. So serene.

I remember sitting there being all calm and still crying and wondering what was wrong with me, so I had a crisis call with my Healer colleague. She reminded me of my own Dreaming and Oneness. That big breath out and that 'aha', OOOHH moment in that same breath. Oh my God. I have made it, I am Oneness, I am:

Feeling it.

Being it.

Doing it.

Thinking it.

Hearing it.

Seeing it.

I am Peace, and I am my safe. I am my sacred.

I had stopped running and, like the brave warrior woman, made sure I could stand still, stand my ground and be found by peace and, importantly, find myself. I have arrived.

Take a long look into my eyes, for they are the Souls of my Ancestors. I am fierce – a warrior woman, a fighter, a survivor, a proud Aboriginal woman of Australia, and I have gracefully carried my own personal trauma story and that of this country of my people. My Dreaming here is to journey, connect, heal and bring people – including myself – back home to their Self, Spirit, heart and breath with grace, honour and peace to feel Oneness.

I dream and wish for my Elders to be at complete peace and have freedom from their trauma stories before they pass over and move on into the Dreamtime. I have not witnessed this yet in my lifetime and hoping one day I can hear the new healing stories of our brave Elders and my people. One day. But until then, I will cast an invisible healing cloak surrounding them and my community for healing love, peace and freedom. I will do this today and every day and continue to rise up and hope and heal until their Spirits are free and healed, and they too are home.

Twisties

During my journey, I began learning and training in a new healing technique – integrating it into my personal practice firstly and then sharing with others. One such technique was Emotional Freedom Technique EFT or tapping as it is known. I was interested in this as ideal for people to self-regulate and self-implement.

I attended with a close colleague, and we both supported each other through the training and processes.

Throughout the four days, we learned many processes and one will last with me and touched me deeply.

The following day we were to bring along a food that we have a passion for or addiction to.

I thought, well, maybe Twisties for me. At the supermarket I couldn't find any, so instead I found a box of Cheezels as they smelled and tasted the same for me anyhow.

During the training and as a group, we tapped and talked, and I was first in line to talk about my food. I talked about how I loved Twisties but only ate them when I felt so depressed, sad, lonely and upset. It soothed me and made me feel loved and comforted.

Going through the process and tapping a few rounds, I suddenly became overwhelmed and emotional. A deep vision and vital memory came up.

While pregnant with my firstborn and having morning sickness most of the way through, Twisties seemed the only thing that could soothe me, and I could eat at times.

Through tapping, I recalled that while pregnant and being in love for the first time and having my own new family, I connected this with the time when I was a young child having my only birthday party ever surrounded and celebrated by my family and that famous favourite moment when I was presented with the big bowl of Twisties and the hidden lollipops.

Wisdom Whisper

Allowing yourself to be brave and being ready to receive the healing and guidance, hear the Ancestors calling your name and reminding you that you are love.

We don't have to hide any more and continue in the darkness.

I learned we are not lost. We are just returning. And that can scare the shit out of you.

- What does your 'being brave' look and feel like?

- What does safe mean?

- Can you vision yourself in a sacred safe space, and what would that be?

Oneness.

*It is the peace, tranquillity and
spirituality that is at One.*

*It is the strength of a
new beginning.*

WHAT DO YOU MEAN
BE GROUNDED?

May you connect and be grounded to Mother Earth while you walk on this Sacred Land.

My preference and calling for groundedness is elemental, and Earth Medicine is my healing practice and teaching. I live my life, and practise and embody this simply to BE (YUMA) Self, Spirit and Mother Earth. A strong part of my YUMA healing practice, for example, is when I create my Spirit Cloths, the nature infusion, essence and bush energy that holds unique healing properties for grounding.

As I sit and gaze out the glass doors and windows, watching the speckles of water fall from the sky, I witness the magic in the raindrops landing on the leaves and trees and forming natural baubles glowing and shining in the light, like a Christmas tree. I observe the leaves flow and move and dance in the slight breeze. I gaze in a new direction, and I see a canopy of ancient trees for as far as my eye can see. It feels very serenely beautiful. Looks like glitter or sparkles being sprayed from the heavens to Mother Earth through this amazing natural wonderland. I see the friendly cockatoo that has been watching and visiting me during my visit here, writing this story, perched under a branch hiding from the rain. He is home and just doing his thing. What I am experiencing and witnessing here evokes a deep sense of what I call and feel is a groundedness. I'm just here in the now and being present, gazing out the window.

The cold air crept in, and the fire was lit. The realization that it was the first day of autumn and felt it was like a celebration and blessing in the new season. Just being here watching the crackling flames dance calmed me into the night.

As I continue to hear the raindrops land harder on the tin roof, I look back out to the canopy of trees to my right and the rain shower of the gods that glides and flows through the trees and lands below gives life on our Mother Earth.

A day after the rain, I was guided to visit the mineral springs, and on arrival, three Yellow-tailed Black Cockatoos welcomed me and flew around me overhead before perching on the tree opposite the park.

My heart was so happy to experience this because, many years earlier, at the beginning of my writing journey of *The Future Ancestor*, I was visited by a whole family of these magical birds, which is very rare.

In Aboriginal Dreaming stories, the Yellow-tailed Black Cockatoo represents a powerful spiritual symbol of Spirit strengthening, change, growth and emotional freedom, joy, contentment and the coming rain.

I felt these amazing birds spoke to my Soul as they flew over me. It symbolized a blessing and honouring of the significant healing growth I have achieved and reached emotionally and spiritually, and the freedom I was experiencing and flowing into. Jumping free of that trauma cage (Tweety-bird).

Even at this very moment, as I am just sitting and being here writing this, I can hear these birds calling out the window and through the trees that back on to the park, which I visited earlier. Oh, this is wonderful, and I feel emotional and proud. And I am reminded of my earlier message.

> *'There is no separation. There is no division.*
> *We have a feeling, and that is our knowing.'*

After the greeting and blessing from the birds, I could feel a strong vibrational pull, and I followed the wind. I arrived at an ancient tree that stopped me in my tracks. I could do nothing more but sit and stare and close my eyes and hear the tree sing healing energy through me. Healing and grounding me in this peaceful stillness.

The tree showed me who I was, from the ancient Ancestors. I could feel there was a strong welcoming connection under the earth of the deep, deep roots that entwined with my Ancients in a further land. I imagined and saw the connecting roots when I embraced the tree and closed my eyes. Sitting in peace here for a while, which seemed like I was in my own magical show with no others invited. The place is usually crowded and busy, but today was my private paradise.

Just a moment in time.

So, what does being grounded mean?

For me, it is all the above, and particularly venturing out into the bush and the natural environments of the lands where I am placed more often, because a deeper connection and relationship with Mother (Earth) is my way of life. It has become so strong as I have healed and also has healed me in ways to make me stronger and allowed peace and freedom to be a part of my intimate life.

I can sit at my own table alone, be alone in the bush, by the river, have a meal alone, dance, sing and be joyful alone. Be in ceremony and ritual alone. For me, this is being grounded, and as time goes on, it becomes easier and more necessary.

Being grounded allows me to be in balance in what I call YUMA, and that is to simply **Be Self, Spirit and Mother Earth** so I can live my unique ONENESS.

Take notice if you feel in balance when you are:

- Being in stillness

- Listening to the land

- Being in the elements

- Animals

- Plants, trees and nature

If you feel uneasy, unsettled or out of balance, it may be that your Spirit needs the most grounding. You could:

Sit by the river, turn your phone off and just watch the ripples flow or the rainfall. It's just water.

Smell the plants, feel and explore the magic and Medicine they offer.

Observe the animals; they are all Spirit animals and may have a unique message for you. Just observe.

Stop running, be present and just BE.

Take your shoes off and feel Mother Earth beneath you.

HOW WILL I KNOW?

I had a Dream.

One day.

Some day.

Any day.

Today.

Every day.

I can walk, breathe, feel and Be peace.

To experience a state of Being – that just is.

To feel this fullness, expansion, and wholeness.

And a deep strength and purity and stillness.

To embody all this and more.

But to feel nothing at all. It just is.

To just Be.

This is the feeling of YUMA that I journey to – have experienced. It is Oneness.

I will start now, today and each day after.

To Be.

To dream.

To believe.

Feel, hear, see.

To embody all I know and all I can be.

I am the Medicine and the light, stars, moon, sky, Mother Earth.

Be the Future Ancestor.

Trust me, you will know when it happens. It may shock you, challenge you, confuse you and scare you just as it has me. But you will know. You have been led on this healing path. Or you are about to if you are reading this book.

Through my career and being a healing practitioner for others and myself, it has become very clear we cannot outrun or run away from our freedom, healing, and peace. It will haunt us and make us unwell, just as I described in my personal experiences earlier, and keep us trapped in that oppressive, dark and unhealthy place.

We are our own Healers and our own Medicine when we just let us BE.

Stop running, hiding. Tell your own story your way.

Turn up the volume and stoke that fire and allow those flames to ignite that journey that is needed for you to feel connected, safe, sacred, peace, love and free. You are worthy, you are your Ancestors' story, and you are, too, a Future Ancestor.

My wish for you is that you will feel the change of peace and love invade your inner Being. You will just BE it and can find and become your safe, sacred, peace and freedom.

YUMA

WISDOM WHISPERS

Be Your Own Healer

A s I drive, the early morning sky is glowing deep red, and I see a slither of the sun opening the sky and about to peek its way through. I breathe in so long and hard I am mesmerized. The trees go by, and the birds fly with eagerness to start the day also. I feel in awe and awake and alive. I'm driving to the nearby town for a naturopath consultation. I have a strong sense of belonging and being in control and empowered.

I am turning up for myself.

I am being my own Healer.

I am saving myself.

This may be and look different for lots of people. When we show up for ourselves and make a decision to create positive change for our wellness, wellbeing, health and existence then we are being our own Healer. Reading that book; going for a health check; doing yoga; going for a walk; meditating; learning a new skill, course or practice; or going on a retreat or workshop. Talking and learning from your Elders about the Old Ways, Bush Medicine and plants. That is what it means to be your own Healer.

For the first time in my life, I visited a naturopath to research ideas for a health issue. It was the greatest gift I gave myself and opened up a new understanding for me.

My ultimate goal will be to create sustainability and be a part of an exchange of energy that does not necessarily mean to exchange money for service. You may know someone who can exchange a healing offering. Call it in, put it out there or find a circle or group, a gathering to be a part of. Being your own Healer does not have to mean being alone or on your own.

- What does it mean to be your own Healer?

- How would you feel?

- What can you do to be your own Healer?

PART FIVE

Home

This section is made up of the following chapters. In this final section, you, the reader, will be invited to dream into a new way of Being and becoming and living the Future Ancestor.

Being home and what that means for you personally, spiritually, emotionally, physically and energetically.

- Will I Love Me Now?

- New Way of Being

- Future Ancestor

As the Spirit Weaver, returning to our *Natural State of Being* should be your PURPOSE.

BE your Purpose.

BE your Reason.

BE your own Healer and the Medicine.

It's simple, really.

Don't play out your Dreaming story through others or allow others to hijack yours.

It really is simple acts of returning kindness back to Self with a dash of love, hope, courage, intention, faith and grace.

> *'To remember our Oneness, we are asked to go beyond the veils created by Generations of forgetting.'*
> JAMIE SAMMS, 1999

WILL I LOVE ME NOW?

For me to arrive home, I had to do some deep, deep inner healing and living and hoping and Dreaming. Most of all, accepting. Accepting Self, accepting my love for Self, and loving Self. Every part of me. Some days, and to be honest, at times it was most days, I felt far from this definition of Home. I felt lost, alone and full of dread. If I did not surrender and call on Spirit and allow Spirit to guide me back home, I would, I'm sure, still feel like I was dying.

Although I say I felt lost, I do know that being lost is a journey. As I tell my clients, 'You are just returning.' This is so true. We must believe there is something new, a change, a better future and healed life.

Growing up, I can – and many people will probably – remember being told, teased or criticized for being too pretty, 'dolling up' as I have heard many times in my family and community. Often these words can be harmful and leave a scar that dulls your love for Self.

Through my community and others I have worked in through my career, I have experienced what my aunty would often call 'crabs in the bucket' – the putting down of looks, confidence and self-esteem of many girls and women. 'Why are you dolling up! Who you trying be! Think you're better than everyone else! Love yourself much!' This form of putting down is actually called 'lateral violence' here in Australia. But over and over, I see how this destroys confidence and self-worth and love. As an Aboriginal person in Australia, it deeply affects identity and our cultural safety. As if we are not marginalized enough in this country, we as a culture have to acknowledge that this kind of damaging behaviour creates issues around self-worth and self-love, and harms a sense of belonging for many.

When we can become the Masters of our own healing through education, learning and loving ourselves all over again, it truly is a wonderful and blessed feeling and experience.

Will I love me now? This is a question that I have asked Self over and over. Growing up, as mentioned, LOVE was not a part of my language; I hadn't heard it before and was often criticized for 'loving Self' too much growing up.

We can also ask:

- What is love anyway?

- What does love feel like, smell like and taste like?

- What has love got to do with anything?

- Can we survive without love?

As an orphan who lost her parents as a toddler, I always wondered, did my parents love me, did they love each other and what was their story?

A number of years ago, and after many breakdowns and breakthroughs, I chose healing. I was drawn to this crystal shop, which you may have read earlier. I walked through this corridor; it truly was like I was in another realm, like heaven. The Healer said to me, 'There is a lady here with a floral dress on and a man.'

The floral dress is what my mother had worn in most of the photos I have of her with the family and where she is nursing me. The man was my father – a Māori man. The Healer describes and details moments. The moments of love they shared together. Dancing and embracing in the kitchen together. In sync and rhythm as one. Moving through life together, sharing love and honouring each other and their home shared with family. Simple moments. But deep everlasting memories that were now being recounted for me in this moment of my healing and questioning life and my own self-worth and love. I then know I was loved deeply and from here have never questioned this again. I felt their love in that dream-like room; it infused into my being so gently and lovingly that it filled me up and reminded me who I am and why I am here. I was created of and from love. I was now feeling my body and Spirit and energy becoming a deeper love. My heart was cracked open further and deeply. And closer to home with them embracing me in that energetic love from then on. A higher love that washes over me when I need it most and helps me draw strength to continue this journey of life and Oneness. I hear these gentle whispers that I will share with you.

Love you, as I love you.

See you, as I see you.

Honour you, as I honour you.

Own and heal your story.

> *'...sometimes we forget where home and our*
> *sacred space is... it's within us...'*

Where and what is HOME, you may be wondering. I am on the final chapter, and often myself wondered what this is about and why was I guided to write this.

Home, in every sense of the word, can be and is messy.

Our physical home of residence can mirror our sense of home in our energetic Spirit, and Soul energy and physical body. For me, I have come to find this to be true.

And I have realized through my working career and my own personal growth and healing that we are mirrors.

Through my journey over the past eight years or so, I have been in this deep cocoon or cave. I feel I was here, but I was not.

Incubating. With these intuitive ripples flowing and keeping me alive.

Just as I have written earlier in this book about how I felt like shit and full of this dark, murky energy that was and felt like I was being poisoned, called trauma.

My physical home became a mirror for this, literally full of shit and dark and murky energy and trauma. A family dog literally shat all over our home. Living in a home for 25-plus years and growing your children there eventually becomes full of stuff. Too much stuff, messy stuff, toxic stuff. Sense of being trapped or caged just like the 'Tweety-bird'.

I did not see this at first. It took a long time to witness this myself. My healing energy was so consumed out of the home, working and building my business and working in the community. Cleansing, purifying my energy and Self for them to continue the work.

But never for this home within myself! Or my physical home. It was like I was not there.

It created disconnection, sadness, at times toxic energy and then a sickness or trauma. My physical body became stuck, I could not consume the goodness my body needed, and this went on for years of having medication that did not shift or make a difference. I could feel the murky shitty stuff rising physically and energetically, desperately wanting and needing to shift and clear and unblock. Resulting in a hospital visit in the city to have a cleansing procedure and to investigate any further deep harm.

Around the same time, a series of events began starting with the pipes blocking so bad – literally, we had shit flowing up the pipes and down the driveway! Resulting in some work by the plumbers to reach the deep root cause. Our much-loved fruit trees being ripped from the ground and disposed of.

Soon after, a house fire next door with flames raging like I have never seen before.

Wild storms like a mini tornado over my town blew the power from our home then flooded the house from below and above. Short-circuiting the main necessary appliances.

Wow, what a mess. I reflect on this now and feel all these shocking elemental events that affected my home were somehow healing my home at the same time. Almost like a big fucking defibrillator shocking and resuscitating my home back to life.

Clearing, cleansing and renewing all that needed to be healed.

Just as I was, and felt, and was experiencing in my physical body through this time.

During this time, I was connecting strongly with Mother Earth for my own healing and cultural practices and have creating a YUMA Healing Practice, which is all deeply based in the elements and Earth Medicine.

I was and still am weaving myself back home thread by thread. Importantly those threads are made of love, all in every sense of the word. And it feels damn good and safe, and finally, I can experience a peace and freedom that I have never witnessed or have become before in my lifetime.

Life's Tapestry

Together we are woven into the fabric that is our life experiences. We are all interwoven. We are all threaded together into the story that is the Oneness.

Together we form the tapestry of life.

NEW WAY OF BEING

As we travel home and are flowing through the healing with grace and honour, every footstep, every breath, every hop, skip and jump, we arrive, and we become closer and closer to home.

Sometimes we have to also be brave and honest to forgive the judgement of others and, importantly, from our own selves.

We can become love.

We gain strength and stability, and we become free.

Our hearts expand and become more peaceful.

Our minds become clear, and our bodies feel normal. Sometimes a feeling of emptiness which creates room for a new flow of energy that fills you up with all that you need to be safe, peaceful and free and, most of all, love.

To be honest, as I am writing this final section, 'Home', I still wait for something bad to happen. I catch myself about to revert to old destructive patterns. I quickly and swiftly kick my own arse. I also sometimes find excuses to delay, cancel or just give up, telling myself I am not good enough, my story is not important, I am not mystical enough. Because that is easier, I used to once think, 'Annabelle, here you are. You have worked and healed and moved through mountains of grief and trauma and created new foundations for change and peace, and here you are rolling and pushing yourself back down the mountain, ready to roll through sabotage again!' What the actual fuck!!

When I catch and hear myself saying that to Self... I know. I am love, and this destructive belief will not be my reality.

Oneness is a way of being that transcends the mind and physical planes.

In Oneness, we are connected with everything in existence

We are one.

It is fullness, infinite expansion and wholeness.

This is a new way of Being.

How do we walk in these new footsteps and continue to create that safe sacred space and energy that we need to maintain this new way?

If we question this over and over again, we may realize we are already doing it. Every action, every breath and every piece of new learning that you have pulled into your energy field has brought you here. You are already doing it.

If you are reading this book, you are already doing it.

I hear from clients a lot, 'I will change tomorrow or next week. I will start doing these things that will change my life.' I gently remind them that they are already doing it. They have turned up. Not for me but for themselves.

You are already doing it. And you need to acknowledge, honour and celebrate that. Don't wait for others to notice or celebrate that in you. Because while you are waiting, you may be waiting for their judgement because that is most likely what you are used to. We are breaking cycles and disrupting the patterns and systems of oppressive destruction of our being, Spirit and life.

We are manifesting change. We are becoming change, and the sooner you own that, you can flow through life with this new energy and become who you are meant to be and not feel lost.

A motion of connection.

A movement of healing.

A continual breath.

A Oneness.

Oneness.

It is the unfurling of fear and conditioning and the recoiling of love, Ancestors, heart, Soul, and YUMA.

A new life and purity to each and every one of us.

It is the peace, tranquillity and spirituality that is at One.

It is the strength of new beginnings.

It is our personal growth, positive change and awakening.

This is where I will further introduce you to my YUMA Healing practice, which has been written about through the book and through the Spirit Cloth.

I need to once again acknowledge my grandmother, Emily, who turned up in my dire need to show, lead and guide and heal me. She shone a bright light on the word YUMA. I was asking Spirit more and more for guidance. I guess I was also testing my own abilities and strengths as a Healer and wanting justification for Self that I was being authentic. Or, importantly, if I was good enough! I was at that stage in my business offering Gathering retreats, and often they were bush camps. Many women from the city travelled to attend.

The word YUMA in my Mutti Mutti language word means 'BE'.

At these gatherings and retreats, I came to quickly realize that is what I was promoting and encouraging through healing – to just BE – To simply BE. Women questioned often, 'But how, why? That seems too simple.' Women who were often very busy Healers and practitioners in their own lives but were obviously drawn to and were searching for something that was missing or overlooked.

Sitting around campfires with pots of Spirit Cloths brewing, I was guided and called to remind these women that they must be their own Healers and Medicine. We are not and cannot be silent in this journey any more. We are here, and we are the Future Ancestors.

Through the YUMA Spirit Cloth is a healing ceremony for individuals to birth and alchemize their Medicine. A beautiful spiritual and healing gathering time together for the higher good and humanity.

Therefore, since my YUMA Healing practice and philosophy has birthed, and this *Future Ancestor* book is being created and written, it has cast a wide, far-reaching net to inspire many humans. It is calling in people who have all the self-development, empowerment and spiritual books. Therapists, Healers and practitioners who care and nurture many and sometimes are triggered, forget to love themselves and lose their way to their own practices, self-care and home. People who have experienced trauma and intergenerational trauma. People who have not had these traumatic experiences, however, have a deep empty feeling in their beings. People who believe they are missing something from life and not sure what. People who want to be better Humans to live in this new, ever-changing world.

YUMA is about being open to be guided and inspired to journey to healing, uncover, unravel, discover a piece of who they truly are, their purpose, love, and find and live Oneness.

To fully embody the meaning To BE Self, Spirit and Mother Earth.

To BE your own Healer and Medicine.

As the Spirit Weaver, my Dreaming is to journey, connect, heal and bring people back home to their own Self, Spirit, heart and breath with grace, honour and peace so they may feel Oneness and live and practise YUMA.

YUMA empowers you to BE your Own Healer and BE the Medicine in your personal Healing, Wellness and Dreaming Journey.

YUMA is a Mutti Mutti language word meaning BE, and YUMA is my Dreaming to live in Oneness, to live and BE Self, Spirit and Mother Earth.

FUTURE ANCESTOR

You, found in the tree that held you, in the strength of your Ancestors' arms.

My message about being a Future Ancestor is not just about me being an Australian Aboriginal person, my people or being a grandmother or for my grandchildren. It's about how we can all be better people and live in a new world, a better world.

We are all Future Ancestors, and as Future Ancestors we each have a responsibility to nurture, protect and restore the balance to our Mother (Earth). We are of her. She owns Us. This Book honours her and honours us.

As a Future Ancestor that honours and lives in Oneness, I embody a healing way practice and breathe with my Soul and the same breath as my Ancestors. I am Always Being, and in tune with Spirit, stars, moon and am at one and in sync with Mother, which is flowing through me with every footstep I take, and I pay deep gratitude and honour her always culturally, spiritually, energetically and physically.

I particularly love the moments when I feel the sweet, gentle embrace and whispers of my Ancestors surrounding me.

To feel Oneness, see Oneness, hear Oneness, breathe Oneness, live Oneness,

Be Oneness.

This book is a gift for all people, all walks of life, cultures, professions, experiences and story.

This book, *The Future Ancestor*, is for humanity.

Star Bright

As I sit under the disappearing sunset that fades into night sky, the first shining star catches my attention.

When I see this star, it feels like a beacon of light. Safety. Home. Oneness.

A light to remind us that all is OK; the universe sees us and hears us and feels our joy and our pain. Hears our cry and our calls. And, importantly, our heartbeat.

*We are all Future Ancestors,
and as a Future Ancestor we
each have a responsibility to
nurture, protect, restore the
balance to our Mother (Earth).*

We are of Her.

She owns Us.

*This book honours her
and honours us.*

When we look to the night sky, we can imagine our Ancestors are there just watching over us. I know they are. I feel them with every breath. A reminder to all.

They will be here tomorrow and the next day and all the days after.

Keep breathing, keep Dreaming, keep being brave. Be the warrior of our Ancestors.

Tell the stories that need to be told and should be told, and we all need to hear.

We sit in and are part of this big universe that revolves rhythmically and in perfect sync, balance and harmony on a daily basis, moment by moment.

We have to decide how we want to move in it, with it, how we move and stay in balance and sync.

We need to strive to stay in balance and harmony, just like the universe we are part of. This big universe that we can sometimes forget we belong to.

Just look up next time after sunset, and the stars shine to remember.

*When I look up to the night sky, I know that
BIAIMI, the great Creator, is holding and protecting
me. I feel hope, I feel I belong, I feel love.*

I am a part of Creation, and one day I will be looking over my future generations of grandchildren. Their Future Ancestor.

*And all in one breath, we are one, we are
everything, and we are nothing but Oneness.*

I can dance and hear the ancient songs through my body and Spirit, and with each footstep, I gain strength and feel free. I heard this now, and I remember.

I am free.

I am life.

I am the future.

I am the Ancestor.

Throughout this book, *The Future Ancestor: A Guide and Journey to Oneness,* I have shared highlights from my personal journey through healing. As I write the final chapter, I feel healed and lived and loved. Shedding and resolving trauma, guilt, and shame.

Finding a beautiful peacefulness, a rooted stability that anchors me and grounds me and wellness that ensured I find positive, healthful new ways of living.

Clearing intergenerational trauma has been a lifelong lived event, and the prize is I now have gained a deep generational strength. I feel it in and through my body and Spirit and every walking waking moment here on Mother Earth in this lifetime that will be paid forward and carried through generations to come.

> *Our Ancestors didn't survive us to be silenced, to hide and to continue to live in trauma, hate and shame and oppression.*
>
> *They have survived through us, all of us.*
>
> *We must rise up to remember, reclaim, regenerate.*

My guided encouragement and lessons are that we must:

- Heal.

- Love from our centre.

- Honour our stories and tell the truth to raise awareness and understanding through sharing and conversations.

- Create and allow safe spaces to hear the stories of pain and trauma.

- Promote and practice respect.

- Encourage hope.

- Approach with fairness and kindness.

- Own our personal integrity – you know what that is.

- Value uniqueness and differences.

- Challenge racism and discrimination.

- Feed Mother Earth with love.

- Be sustainable.

- Pay reverence to the Ancestors and land in which we stand.

- Find our unique Oneness.

- Find our Medicine and claim the warrior for peace, freedom, healing and our sacred.

- Gain the Ancestral strength of Connection to live Self, Spirit and Mother Earth.

This book has been a mourning and a celebration at the same time. A revealing and shocking meeting of truths and trauma and a greeting of Ancestral connection, wisdom, and cultural strength.

Just as Mother Earth is alive, so am I; my being is – my skin, my cells, my heartbeat and altogether in Oneness and in sync. Know your poison, whatever that may be. Untangle and unravel yourself to allow its toxic and damaging hold of you. Heal it, Release it. Do no more harm.

For me to be a Future Ancestor it is all the above and now I can finally BE Oneness, practise and share my Medicine and that is YUMA and the Spirit Cloth.

> *YUMA is seeking and being this Delicate Strength to Ancestral Connectedness, to be a Future Ancestor, a Returning, an Earthing, a Knowing and Being.*

Yumila Kiyaka.

In Oneness.

YUMA

WISDOM WHISPERS

Be the Medicine

You are the Dreaming of your Ancestors, and when all is in balance and you are being Self, Spirit and Mother Earth and become your own Healer, you are the Medicine.

A unique and embodied life force living Oneness.

My Human vessel has been cradling YUMA whispers for 50 years.

I heard them when I was born and throughout my early childhood.

Memories.

Moments.

These Whispers have become louder as I have grown.

They are the universe, stars, moon, and sky.
The land, water, trees, animals, wind and fire.
My Ancestors' heartbeats and breath.

The whispers are wisdom and knowledge, a deep knowing.

A Being. To Be, a Oneness. This is what I call YUMA.

To BE Self, Spirit and Mother Earth. So, I can Live in
Oneness. Experience Oneness and Be Oneness.

My grandmother Emily revealed and guided me to this word YUMA (meaning BE in Mutti Mutti language). To heal myself, first I had to embody YUMA.

Story, love, Spirit, Soul, culture and the Ancients.

That has held me in this lifetime, this human experience.

They arrive through me, my feeling, seeing, hearing, singing, my voice, my writing, they are me.

That's my gold. My gift, my mystical. Most importantly, they have nurtured me when I needed it most and often when I was not aware. Guided and healed me in ways I thought not possible. Saved me. My Medicine.

My Ancestors. Aboriginal Peoples of this country, Australia, and Māori from across the waters. Strong ancient lineages, culture, customs, story, knowledge, wisdom and healing ways.

My daughters once teased some workshop guests and told them I only married their father, my husband, for his name! They were not aware my last name was Sharman, and thought it just the name of the business – A SHARMAN HOPE HEALING.

As you read, I write about my theory or a knowing that my Mother's Spirit chose my husband, Bruce, for me. True story.

On the other hand, I had been told a few years back while I sat on my Mutti Mutti country by a white woman who is a Healer, that I cannot be or practise as a 'shaman' because I have not been to Peru!

'Ummm, what is a shaman?' I say. It's a question I also asked other colleagues at the time. It wasn't a word or part of my language or meaning.

I thought, *I just is! I am, I Be. I carry 80,000-plus years of this GOLD*, as I mentioned before. And I haven't left Robinvale. My home in Mallee bush along the Murray River.

Thank you, Mum, for choosing my man and thanks, Bruce Sharman, for showing up and loving me and also sharing your name with me.

The Future Ancestor: A Guide and Journey to Oneness.

My story. Many may find it is their story too. As the story weaves its way through the pages, my hope is you are guided to find you, your Medicine, Dreaming, Healing and Oneness.

The Live in Oneness Blessing

BE Self, Spirit and Mother Earth.

Let your journey continue here.

*Allow your Spirit to explore, and
imagination run wild and free.*

*May you be inspired and empowered
to share, learn, love.*

*May you connect and be grounded to Mother
Earth while you walk on this Sacred Land.*

BE still, present and connect.

*May you be blessed on your journey
to continue your Dreaming and be
empowered to BE your own Healer and
BE the Medicine to Live in Oneness.*

ANNABELLE SHARMAN